india
esse

ATUL KOCHHAR

PHOTOGRAPHS BY DAVID LOFTUS

indian essence

THE FRESH TASTES OF INDIA'S NEW CUISINE

whitecap

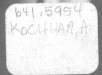
To my beautiful baby daughter Amisha

Publishing director Anne Furniss
Art director Helen Lewis
Project editors Janet Illsley and Carole Clements
Senior designer Jim Smith
Photographer David Loftus
Food stylist Atul Kochhar
Props stylist Jane Campsie
Production Beverley Richardson

First published in the U.S. and Canada in 2004 by

Whitecap Books
351 Lynn Avenue
North Vancouver
British Columbia
Canada, V7J 2C4

ISBN 1 55285 568 6
Printed and bound in China

NOTES

- All recipes serve 4 as part of an Indian meal featuring a selection of
  dishes, unless otherwise indicated.
- Ingredients highlighted with an asterisk are explained in the glossary
  on pages 156–7.
- All spoon measures are level unless otherwise stated: 1 tsp = 5 ml spoon;
  1 tbsp = 15 ml spoon.
- Use fresh herbs unless dried herbs are suggested.
- Use sea salt and freshly ground black pepper unless otherwise stated.
- All vegetables and fruit should be washed and peeled as normal.
- Ovens and broilers must be preheated to the setting specified in the recipe.

I would like to thank the Almond Board
of California very much for all their help
and support during this exciting project.

CONTENTS

INTRODUCTION

Indian food is as diverse as its culture, geography, and climate. It is vibrant, colorful, enticing, easy to prepare, and wonderfully satisfying. The essence of good Indian cooking revolves around the appropriate use of aromatic spices. Spicing is not a difficult concept. In the same way that salt and pepper are used in the west, the skill lies in using spices to enhance, rather than overwhelm the intrinsic flavor of a particular dish.

From a young age, an Indian child is exposed to an extraordinary array of flavor combinations, probably more so than in any other civilization. Indian cuisine is based on a variety of flavor sensations that encompasses hot and sour, hot and nutty, sweet and hot, bitter and hot, bitter and sour, to name but a few. In seasoning, it ranges from the fresh, sweetness of aromatic curry leaves to the dark pungency of the resin, asafoetida. Indian genius lies not only in combining seasonings, but also in drawing out several flavors from a single spice – by roasting, grinding, or frying – to create a vast spectrum of flavors.

Indians are adventurous and there is nothing that cannot be spiced up in an Indian kitchen, but it is important to understand the distinction between spice and heat. In India, heat is generally applied with chilies and selectively, whereas spicing is all about flavoring. In the south, chili heat is valued for its ultimate cooling effect on the body, by inducing perspiration. In the north, dishes are not overly hot – it's all about bringing out the best of the spices. Though, of course, there are always pickles and chutneys to impart fiery heat if required.

Indian ingredients and spices are relatively easy to source these days. Most supermarkets now stock a good range of spices and ethnic ingredients, and Indian food stores, offering fresh vegetables and fruits, as well as specialist dried foods, are ever more abundant. If you do not have an Indian food store or well stocked supermarket nearby, surf the net for a mail order alternative – you will find several specialist Indian food suppliers. You may also be able to buy ingredients in delicatessens and other gourmet food stores. Many Egyptian, Iranian, and Moroccan ingredients, for example, are similar to Indian items.

Religious and regional influences

Religion is said to be the most important aspect of Indian life and food its most precious resource. The majority of Indians are vegetarian due to their belief in Hinduism, Jainism, or Buddhism. Certain foods are deemed pure or sacred and feature prominently in temple rituals. Food also plays an important role in the numerous festivals and ceremonies across the subcontinent. Often a festival is associated with a particular food – sweet semolina pancakes, for example, are synonymous with *holi*, the festival of color.

Although a number of religions exist in India, the two cultures that have influenced Indian cooking and food habits more than any other are the Hindu and Muslim traditions. Each new wave of settlers brought with them their own culinary practices. However, over time, they adopted specialities and cooking techniques from the Indian cuisine and merged them with their own to perfection. The Portuguese, Persians, and British made important contributions to the Indian culinary scene. For example, it was the British who started the commercial cultivation of tea in India.

The Hindu vegetarian custom is widespread in India, although many Hindus now eat meat. The Muslim tradition is most evident in the cooking of meats. *Mughlai* food, *kebabs*, rich *kormas* (curries), and *nargisi koftas* (meatballs), *biryani*, *rogan josh*, and preparations from the clay oven or *tandoor*, like *tandoori rotis* and *tandoori* chicken, are contributions from the Muslim settlers in India.

As India is such a vast country, food customs vary from region to region. The north is the culinary heart of India, with Delhi at the hub, and this was the first regional cuisine to set foot outside India. The food is rich and colorful, and the spicing is generally very aromatic. Wheat is the staple food and *roti* (bread) is served at every meal. A typical north Indian meal would consist of *chapattis* (unleavened bread baked on a griddle) or *parathas* (unleavened bread fried on a griddle), rice, and an assortment of dishes like dals, fried vegetables, curries, paneer, chutney, and pickles. Most north Indian desserts are similar in taste as they are derived from a milk pudding or rice base and are usually soaked in syrup. *Kheer*, a form of rice pudding, and *kulfi*, a nutty ice cream, are typical northern desserts.

South India comprises Andhra Pradesh, Tamil Nadu, Karnataka, and Kerala. The food is generally light, non-greasy, and fragrant with curry leaves, coconut, and spices. Indeed, this is the main region for the production of spices. Rice is the staple food and forms the basis of every meal. It is usually served with *rasam* (soup), *sambhar* (lentil preparation), dry and curried vegetables, and a curd preparation called *pachadi*. Coconut is an important ingredient in south Indian food. *Dosas* (rice pancakes) and *idli* (steamed rice cakes) are now popular throughout the country. *Appams* (rice pancakes) are a Keralan speciality.

The food in the western states – Maharashtra, Gujarat, Rajasthan, Goa, and Madhya Pradesh – varies significantly from state to state. Rajasthan, for example, is known for its robust meat and poultry dishes, while Gujarat is home to superb, fresh tasting and light vegetarian dishes. East India includes some of the poorest states in India, which is reflected in eating habits, but it makes some interesting culinary contributions, notably with its colorful street foods. The cuisine of Bengal is the most influential and interesting, with a combination of Hindu and Muslim foods.

Planning an Indian menu

In Indian homes, menus are planned around a core recipe. For the majority of Indians who are vegetarian, this will be a lentil or other legume. Then two, three, or four vegetable dishes will be chosen to serve with it. These provide contrast in texture, flavor, and color. Rice or bread (or both) will be served alongside, and a dessert rounds off most meals. For non-vegetarians, there may be two core recipes – featuring seafood, poultry, game, or meat – plus two or three vegetables, a lentil dish, rice and/or bread, with a dessert to follow.

Indians are enthusiastic hosts, and entertaining menus are often quite ambitious – almost mini banquets. It is not unusual to serve two or three appetizers, two or three core recipes, perhaps four vegetables, rice, one or two types of bread, and a couple of desserts. Of course, menus differ from region to region. Among non-vegetarians, north Indians are big meat and poultry eaters; west Indians favor lamb, duck, and fish; east Indians like fish, lamb, and poultry; while in the south you find fish, game, meat, and poultry. Of course, vegetarian dishes are an essential part of any meal, so two or three vegetables are chosen, usually a mixture of root, stem, and leafy vegetables for variety.

Although Indians generally prefer to prepare their own regional food, they are adventurous and "pan-Indian" menus featuring dishes from all over the subcontinent are increasingly common. So, when you are choosing dishes for a meal, don't hesitate to mix and match recipes from different regions. For ideas on composing menus, see my suggestions on pages 154–5. There are no hard and fast rules, so feel free to alter these as you please, aiming to offer a rich variety of flavors, colors, and textures – to convey the essence of Indian food.

STARTERS AND SNACKS

In India, eating out is a serious business and that is why café and street food is so huge. When they are out and about, people like to grab something to eat while talking, shopping, browsing, or conducting business. Most of the foods eaten are comparable to western snacks or starters – and Indians will return home for a proper meal after snacking. In this chapter, I have included a melange of street food, café food, railway platform food, beach food, and some traditional regional home cooking. As you would expect, most of the recipes are easy and quick to prepare.

JHAL MURI

Seasoned puffed rice   BIHAR, EAST INDIA

This was once my favorite food and it still brings back memories of my childhood in east India. *Jhal muri* is eaten as a snack, salad, or an appetizer. It is also one of the colorful street foods of eastern India – typically eaten with *channa bhaja* (pressed crisp-fried spicy gram) or *channa choor* (chickpea snack). It is quite close to the *bhel puri* and *sev puri* of western India, but it has an eastern flavor profile. *Jhal muri* can include a wide variety of interesting ingredients, but I have kept the combination relatively simple here.

First make the dressing. Put the mustard oil, lime juice, chili powder, toasted cumin, and mango powder into a small bowl and whisk together until evenly blended. Stir in the tamarind chutney, if using, and season with salt to taste. Set aside.

Put the puffed rice into a large bowl, add the sev, and toss to mix. Add the chopped onion, potato, tomato, cucumber, and green chili pepper. Mix well, then add the shredded cilantro, sprouted beans, and peanuts. Mix all the ingredients together, then add the dressing and toss to mix. Pile the salad into a bowl to serve.

Note: Sev is a ready-made Indian snack, best described as crispy deep-fried chickpea flour noodles flavored with various spices – red chili powder, fenugreek leaf powder, salt, etc. Puffed rice is known by various names, including *muri* in the east and *phuliyan* in the north. Both puffed rice and sev are available from Indian grocery stores and specialist suppliers.

Variation: Use freshly cooked or canned chickpeas instead of the mixed sprouted beans.

8oz Indian puffed rice

2oz sev (vermicelli-like crisp savory noodle snack)

1/2 red onion, finely chopped

1/2 boiled potato, diced

1/2 tomato, finely chopped

1/3 cup cucumber, finely chopped

1 green chili pepper, finely chopped

1 tbsp shredded cilantro leaves

1/2 cup mixed sprouted beans

1/4 cup peanuts, roasted or fried and salted (with skins)

DRESSING:

4 tsp mustard oil

2 tsp lime juice

1/4 tsp Kashmiri red chili powder*

1/4 tsp toasted cumin seeds, crushed

1/4 tsp mango powder*

1 tbsp sweet tamarind chutney (page 138, optional)

1/2 tsp salt, or to taste

PAPARIS RECHEADOS

Stuffed poppadoms   GOA, WEST INDIA

Papads are made from different lentils – the ones made from urad dal are ideal for this recipe. I have filled them with spicy gingery shrimp, but you can use a different stuffing, such as spiced mashed potato. Serve with a salad and a spicy chutney – mango and passion fruit chutney (page 140) goes brilliantly and passion fruit are native to Goa.

To make the stuffing, heat the oil in a frying pan, add the onion, garlic, ginger, and black pepper, and sauté until the onion is softened and translucent. Add the ground coriander, turmeric, and shrimp, sauté for 3–4 minutes, then add the potatoes, lemon juice, and salt. Sprinkle with the chopped cilantro and cinnamon, mix well, and set aside to cool.

Meanwhile, soak the papads in warm water for 5–10 minutes to soften, then drain. Mix the flour with a little water to form a paste. Spoon the shrimp mixture onto one side of the papads, then roll up, folding in the sides, and seal the edges with flour paste.

Heat the oil for deep-frying in a suitable pan to 320°F. Deep-fry the stuffed papads, a few at a time, for 2–3 minutes until crisp and golden. Drain on paper towel and serve hot, with a chutney.

8 plain or spicy papads (uncooked poppadoms)
1 tbsp bread flour or all-purpose flour
vegetable oil, to deep-fry

STUFFING:
1 tbsp vegetable oil
1 large onion, finely chopped
1 tsp finely chopped garlic
1 tbsp finely chopped ginger
1 tsp freshly ground black pepper
1/4 tsp ground coriander
1/2 tsp ground turmeric
7oz peeled raw shrimp, roughly chopped
2/3 cup roughly chopped boiled potatoes
1 tbsp lemon juice
1/2 tsp salt, or to taste
2 tbsp chopped cilantro leaves
ground cinnamon, to sprinkle

TARKARI NI BHAJIA

Parsi vegetable fritters   WEST INDIA

I am a true fan of this *bhaji*. The combination of ingredients and spices – and the unusual method – brings out the flavors to the full. Serve hot, with sweet tamarind chutney (page 138).

For the batter, put the tamarind pulp in a bowl with 4 tbsp warm water and leave to soak for 20 minutes, then strain through a fine strainer.

Parboil the potatoes in salted water for 5–7 minutes, then drain and grate when cool enough to handle. Heat the oil for deep-frying in a suitable pan and deep-fry the onions until lightly caramelized. Remove and drain on paper towel; set aside. (Keep the oil to cook the fritters.)

Put the green chili peppers, cilantro leaves, garlic, dried chili, and 1/2 tsp salt in a blender or mini-processor and whiz to a rough paste; set aside.

For the batter, mix the dry ingredients together in a bowl, then add the tamarind juice and 7 tbsp water, and mix until smooth.

Mash the bananas in a bowl, then add the potatoes and onion and mix well. Mix in the spicy paste, followed by the batter to make a stiff paste.

Heat the oil for deep-frying to 375°F. With a wet spoon, drop in spoonfuls of mixture and deep-fry in batches for 3–5 minutes until golden. Serve hot.

2 medium potatoes, peeled and
     quartered
salt
vegetable oil, to deep-fry
2 medium onions, finely sliced
2 green chili peppers, stems removed
1 tbsp cilantro leaves
4 garlic cloves, peeled
1 dried red Kashmiri chili pepper*
2 ripe bananas, peeled

BATTER:
1 tbsp tamarind pulp*
1 1/4 cups gram flour*
1/2 tsp salt
1/2 tsp baking soda
1/2 tsp ground turmeric

MOMOS

Indian dim sum ARUNACHAL PRADESH, EAST INDIA

Indian dim sum owe their origin to Tibetan influence on tribal Indian food in Arunachal Pradesh. This north-eastern state is predominantly Buddhist and the sixth Dalai Lama was born here. Momos may have either a vegetarian or non-vegetarian stuffing and are often eaten with a grilled tomato chutney and/or sweet tamarind chutney.

Sift the flour and salt into a bowl, make a well in the middle, and add 7 tbsp water. Mix to a smooth, firm dough, then knead in the oil. Wrap in plastic wrap and leave to rest for 1 hour. Meanwhile, mix the stuffing ingredients together in a bowl.

Divide the dough into 10 portions and shape into small balls. With a rolling pin, flatten out each ball to a disk and place 1 tsp of stuffing in the center. Brush the edges of the dough together with water, gather up over the filling, and pinch together to seal and form parcels.

Put the dumplings in a steamer over a pan of boiling stock or water with the bay leaf and ginger added. Cover and steam for 10–12 minutes, until cooked through. Serve hot, with chutneys.

1²/₃ cups bread flour or all-purpose flour
1 tsp salt
1¹/₂ tbsp vegetable oil
stock, flavored with bay leaf and ginger, to steam

STUFFING:
3¹/₂ oz finely ground lean lamb, pork or chicken
¹/₂ tsp Kashmiri red chili powder*
¹/₂ tsp ground coriander
10 basil leaves, chopped
¹/₂ tsp salt
¹/₂ onion, finely chopped
1 green chili pepper, finely chopped

TO SERVE:
grilled tomato chutney (page 139)
sweet tamarind chutney (page 138)

LITTEE

Spicy stuffed baked dough balls BIHAR, EAST INDIA

A speciality of Bihar, *littee* are similar to the *batti* of Rajasthan, and *bafla* of Madhya Pradesh; it is the stuffing that varies. *Littee* use spicy black gram flour, *batti* use spicy green peas, while *bafla* are filled with spicy potato or cornmeal. They are typically eaten with a potato and cauliflower curry (as illustrated on page 109), or dal.

Sift the flour and salt into a bowl, make a well, and add the ginger-garlic paste, green chili paste, and about ³/₄ cup water. Mix well and knead in the 4 tbsp ghee to make a smooth, firm dough. Wrap in plastic wrap and leave to rest for 1 hour. Preheat the oven to 375°F (350°F convection oven).

Meanwhile, mix all the stuffing ingredients together in a bowl with 2 tbsp water to form a rough crumbly mixture, then set aside.

Divide the dough into 12 balls, 2-in diameter. Flatten each one just enough to form a hollow for the stuffing. Put in a heaped teaspoonful of stuffing, bring the dough over to enclose, and roll again to a ball shape.

Place the dough balls on a greased baking tray and bake for 10 minutes. Turn and bake for a further 10 minutes until the littee are golden brown; a few cracks should appear on the surface. Dip into (or brush with) melted ghee and serve hot, with the cauliflower and potato curry.

4 cups bread flour or all-purpose flour
1 tsp salt
2 tsp ginger-garlic paste*
1 tsp green chili paste*
4 tbsp ghee*

STUFFING:
1¹/₄ cups sattu (roasted black gram flour)*
¹/₃ cup finely chopped red onion
2 green chili peppers, finely chopped
1 tbsp cilantro leaves, finely chopped
1 tsp cumin seeds, toasted and crushed
¹/₂ tsp ajwain seeds*
1 tsp finely chopped ginger
¹/₂ tsp salt

TO SERVE:
melted ghee*, to dip or brush
cauliflower and potato curry (page 109)

KARJIKAI

Coorgi vegetable puffs KARNATAKA, SOUTH INDIA

Originating from Coorg, this is another samosa – with a difference in shape and spicing. Similar pastries are made all over India. These are particularly good served with a cucumber salad (page 32).

Sift the flour and salt into a bowl, add 6 tbsp water, and mix until smooth. Knead in the oil to make a pliable dough. Wrap in plastic wrap and leave to rest in the fridge for 30 minutes.

For the stuffing, parboil the potato in salted water for 5–7 minutes; drain, cool slightly, and grate. Heat the oil in a pan and sauté the cumin seeds and curry leaves for 2 minutes. Add chili pepper and ginger; sauté for 1 minute.

Add the carrots and beans, and cook, stirring, for 3 minutes. Add the ground spices and cook for 1 minute. Stir in the potato and peas, and cook for 5–8 minutes until the vegetables are tender. Check seasoning.

Divide the dough into 12 balls and roll each piece into a 4-in diameter round. Put a generous spoonful of stuffing on one side of each round and moisten the dough edges with water. Fold the dough over the filling and press the edges together to seal. Rest the pastries for 15 minutes.

Heat the oil for deep-frying in a suitable pan to 340°F. Deep-fry the samosas, a few at a time, for 3–5 minutes or until golden. Serve hot.

1²/₃ cups bread flour or all-purpose flour

¹/₂ tsp salt

3 tbsp vegetable oil

vegetable oil, to deep-fry

STUFFING:

¹/₂ lb potato, peeled

salt

2 tbsp oil

¹/₂ tsp cumin seeds

6 curry leaves*

1 green chili pepper, finely chopped

1 tbsp finely chopped ginger

1 cup grated carrots

²/₃ cup chopped green beans

¹/₂ tsp each ground coriander, turmeric, and cumin

¹/₂ tsp Kashmiri red chili powder*

²/₃ cup shelled fresh peas

LUQMI

Spicy lamb pastries HYDERABAD, SOUTH INDIA

The word *luqmi* is derived from the Arabic *luqma*, meaning a morsel. Serve with mango and passion fruit chutney (page 140).

Sift the flour and salt into a bowl, add the yogurt and 7 tbsp water, and mix until smooth. Knead in the ghee or oil to make a pliable dough. Wrap in plastic wrap and leave to rest in the fridge for 30 minutes.

For the stuffing, put the lamb, spices, ginger-garlic paste, salt, and 2 cups water in a pan. Bring to a simmer and cook for 30 minutes or until the lamb is cooked and the mixture is dry. Heat the oil in another pan and sauté the chili peppers and cilantro for 1 minute. Add the meat and cook, stirring, for 3–5 minutes. Add the lemon zest and juice; take off the heat.

Divide the dough into 16 pieces. Roll out each one to an oblong 6 in long. Put 2 tbsp stuffing in the middle, moisten the dough edges with water, and fold over to enclose the stuffing and form a rectangle, about 3 x 1¹/₂ in. Press the edges well to seal and trim to neaten.

Heat the oil for deep-frying in a suitable pan to 340°F. Deep-fry the pastries a few at a time for 5–6 minutes until golden brown. Serve hot.

2 cups bread flour or all-purpose flour

1 tsp salt

2 tbsp plain yogurt

4 tbsp ghee* or vegetable oil

vegetable oil, to deep-fry

STUFFING:

1 lb 2 oz lean ground lamb

1 tsp Kashmiri red chili powder*

¹/₂ tsp ground turmeric

1 tbsp ginger-garlic paste*

¹/₂ tsp salt

3 tbsp vegetable oil

4 green chili peppers, finely chopped

2 tbsp chopped cilantro leaves

grated zest and juice of 2 lemons

NIZAMI SUBJ KATHI

Spicy vegetable wrap CALCUTTA, EAST INDIA

This is typical street food in Calcutta, but it is also an excellent snack or starter to prepare at home. The original version, created under Muslim rule in east India, featured meat pan-fried with spices and vegetables, and then rolled in a large *roti* or flat bread. Often this bread was dipped into egg batter and pan-fried first, to keep it moist around the filling. I think my vegetarian version is equally exciting.

First make the filling. Heat the oil in a wok or kadhai, add the cumin seeds, and sauté until they crackle. Add the ginger julienne, green chili pepper, and onion. Sauté gently until the onion is softened and translucent. Add the carrot, cabbage, and mushrooms, and sauté for 1 minute. Add the ground spices and salt, and cook for 2–3 minutes until the vegetables soften slightly. Add the paneer strips and toss to mix. Remove from the heat and allow to cool, then add the lemon juice and chopped cilantro leaves.

To make the batter, put the gram flour, salt, spices, and chopped cilantro into a bowl, and mix well. Add about 5–6 tbsp water and mix to a smooth, thick batter.

To cook the chapattis, heat the 3 tbsp oil in a large frying pan. One at a time, dip the chapattis into the batter and pan-fry for about 1 minute on each side.

To assemble, lay the breads on a clean surface, spoon the filling in to the center, and add some roasted pepper julienne. Roll up to enclose the filling. Serve the wraps warm or cold, garnished with cilantro, and accompanied by mint chutney and a salad (see below).

Cucumber and tomato salad: Toss julienne of cucumber, onion, and tomato in lemon juice with a sprinkling of Kashmiri red chili powder and toasted cumin seeds to serve with this wrap.

4 large chapattis or tortillas

3 tbsp vegetable oil

FILLING:

4 tbsp vegetable oil

1 tsp cumin seeds

1 tsp ginger julienne

1 tsp chopped green chili pepper

1 red onion, thinly sliced

1 carrot, cut into julienne

1 1/3 cups white cabbage, finely sliced or shredded

8 shiitake mushrooms, sliced

1 tsp Kashmiri red chili powder*

1 tsp ground turmeric

1 tsp ground coriander

1/2 tsp garam masala

1/2 tsp salt, or to taste

3 1/2 oz paneer cheese (see note on page 31), cut into strips

1 tbsp lemon juice

2 tbsp chopped cilantro leaves

1/2 cup roasted (or grilled) red bell pepper or pimento, cut into julienne

BATTER:

7 tbsp gram flour*

1/4 tsp salt

1/4 tsp Kashmiri red chili powder

1/4 tsp ground turmeric

1 tbsp chopped cilantro leaves

TO SERVE:

cilantro sprigs, to garnish

mint chutney (page 140)

RAJMA KE GELAWATI

Red kidney bean cakes NORTH INDIA

I first ate these soft, savory cakes in a strict vegetarian house in the city of Benares and was so impressed that I persuaded the family to let me have the recipe. It's an easy recipe with no-fuss ingredients, and the cakes taste superb.

Drain the kidney beans, put into a saucepan, and add the cardamom pod and enough cold water to cover generously. Bring to a boil and boil steadily for 10 minutes, then lower the heat and cook for 1½ hours or until tender, adding salt toward the end of the cooking time.

Drain the beans and place in a blender or food processor with the cumin, chili powder, and coconut. Whiz until smooth, then pour into a bowl.

Add the mint, ginger, and mango powder, and mix well. Finally mix in the bread crumbs and check the seasoning, adding a little more salt if needed. Shape the mixture into cakes, about 2-in diameter and ³/₄-in thick. Place on a tray and refrigerate for 30 minutes.

To cook the cakes, heat a nonstick frying pan or griddle, add the oil, and reduce the heat to medium. Fry the cakes for 3–4 minutes on each side until crisp and browned. Serve hot, with mustard and yogurt chutney.

1¼ cups dried red kidney beans, soaked in cold water overnight
1 black cardamom pod*
1 tsp salt, or to taste
1½ tsp toasted cumin seeds, crushed
1 tsp Kashmiri red chili powder*
2 tbsp toasted unsweetened dried coconut*
2 tbsp chopped mint leaves
1 tbsp chopped ginger
1 tsp mango powder*
2 tbsp fresh bread crumbs
2 tbsp vegetable oil
mustard and yogurt chutney (page 138)

ALOO TIKKI

Pan-fried potato cakes LUCKNOW, NORTH INDIA

The gastronomic city of Lucknow is home to _Chowk ki Tikki_ – a street which is famous for its enticing food. During the Mogul empire, the _Nawab_ rulers of this city spent most of their time promoting art, culture, and food, so Lucknow has a long tradition of courting food. It even has its own cuisine, called _awadhi_. These tasty potato cakes are best served with tomato chutney, but ketchup will do if you are short of time.

Parboil the potatoes in salted water for 5–7 minutes, then drain. When cool enough to handle, peel and grate, then place in a bowl.

Add the spices, ginger, green chili pepper, and chopped cilantro. Mix thoroughly and season with salt to taste.

Shape the mixture into cakes, about 2-in diameter and ³/₄-in thick, and pat well to firm up. Place on a tray and refrigerate for 20 minutes.

To cook the cakes, heat a nonstick frying pan or griddle, add the oil, and reduce the heat to medium. Fry the cakes for 3–5 minutes on each side until crisp and browned. Serve hot, with tomato chutney.

14oz boiling potatoes, peeled and quartered
salt
1½ tsp toasted cumin seeds, crushed
½ tsp Kashmiri red chili powder*
1 tbsp chopped ginger
½ tsp chopped green chili pepper
2 tbsp chopped cilantro leaves
2 tbsp vegetable oil
tomato chutney, to serve (page 139)

SHAMMI KEBAB

Pan-fried lamb cakes — LUCKNOW, NORTH INDIA

The *Nawab* rulers of Lucknow favored these lamb cakes with their interesting blend of meat, lentil, and spices. The rulers of Hyderabad had their own version of *shammi*, called *shikampuri kebab*. The *Nawabs* created all manner of variations and spared no expense with their choice of flavorings. However, this is a simple recipe and one that works well. If you have kewra water* handy, add 1 tsp to the mixture with the chopped herbs to enhance the flavor.

Put the lamb in a pan with the garlic, gram, dried chili peppers, whole spices, ½ tsp salt, and 2 cups water. Bring to a boil, lower the heat, and simmer, uncovered, for about 40 minutes until the meat and gram are cooked and the water has evaporated. Cool slightly, then remove the whole spices if preferred. Put the mixture into a food processor or blender and whiz to a smooth, fine paste.

Put the meat mixture into a bowl and add the onions, ginger, green chilies, and ground spices. Mix thoroughly, add salt to taste, then add the chopped herbs and mix until evenly blended.

Divide the mixture into 14–18 pieces and shape into small round cakes. Place the lamb cakes on a tray and rest in the fridge for 30 minutes.

Heat the oil in a nonstick frying pan over a medium heat. Shallow-fry the lamb cakes, in batches, for about 2–3 minutes on each side. Serve hot, garnished with cilantro sprigs. Accompany with mint chutney, and mango chutney topped with some shredded mango.

1lb 2oz lean ground lamb
5 garlic cloves, peeled
½ cup Bengal gram*
4 dried red Kashmiri chili peppers*
6 black peppercorns
2 black cardamom pods*
1-in piece cassia bark or cinnamon stick
1 tsp salt, or to taste
⅔ cup finely chopped onions
1 tbsp finely chopped ginger
5 green chili peppers, finely chopped
1 tsp garam masala
½ tsp ground mace
½ tsp green cardamom powder*
2 tbsp chopped mint leaves
2 tbsp chopped cilantro leaves
⅔ cup vegetable oil, to shallow-fry

TO SERVE:
cilantro sprigs, to garnish
mint chutney (page 140)
mango chutney (page 140)
a little shredded green mango

MURG KALEJI MASALA

Pan-fried chicken livers — PUNJAB, NORTH INDIA

Chicken livers are highly prized in Punjab – the equivalent to foie gras in France. In local villages a plate of pan-fried chicken livers is often served with drinks in the evening. I like to serve them in toasted poppadoms with a simple cucumber and tomato salad (see page 20).

Cut the chicken livers into 1-in dice and set aside. Heat the oil in a sauté pan and sauté the cumin seeds until they crackle. Add the chopped ginger, then the onion, and sauté until softened.

Add the chicken livers and sauté for 1 minute, then add the mushrooms and sauté for 2 minutes. Add the ground spices and chili powder, and cook, stirring, for 30 seconds. Add the chopped tomato, season with salt, and cook for 1 minute. Stir in the lime juice and remove from the heat.

Serve the chicken livers sprinkled with the chopped cilantro leaves.

7oz chicken livers, trimmed and cleaned
1 tbsp vegetable oil
1 tsp cumin seeds
1 tbsp finely chopped ginger
⅓ cup finely chopped onion
2oz white mushrooms, quartered
¼ tsp ground turmeric
½ tsp ground coriander
½ tsp Kashmiri red chili powder*
1 small tomato, seeded and chopped
½ tsp salt, or to taste
1 tbsp lime juice
1 tbsp chopped cilantro leaves

PASTEIS DE OSTRAS

Oyster turnovers   GOA, WEST INDIA

In Goa, these pastries are filled with all manner of tasty stuffings – based on meat, fish, or vegetables – and they are usually deep-fried rather than baked. I like to serve them with a tomato chutney, or a spicy ketchup.

First make the stuffing. Heat the oil in a sauté pan and sauté the onion until softened. Add the ginger-garlic paste and sauté for 1–2 minutes, then add the green chili pepper and turmeric and sauté for another minute.

Add the peppers with the salt, and sauté until they have softened. Add the reserved oyster juice and white wine. Let bubble until the liquid has evaporated, then add the oysters and sauté for 1 minute. Remove from the heat and set aside to cool.

Preheat oven to 400°F (360°F convection oven). Roll out the pastry to a $^3/_{16}$-in thickness and cut out 4 rounds, 5-in diameter, using a saucer as a guide. Spoon the oyster mixture onto one side of the rounds and brush the pastry edges with egg wash. Fold the pastry over the filling and press the edges together to seal and form half-moon shapes. Brush with egg wash and bake for 8–12 minutes until the pastry is risen and golden brown.

Serve warm, topped with green onion julienne and accompanied by a tomato chutney, and a mixed leaf salad, if you like.

13oz frozen puff pastry, thawed

1 small egg, beaten with 1 tsp water
  (egg wash)

2 cups mixed salad leaves

STUFFING:

1 tbsp vegetable oil

1 large onion, chopped

2 tsp ginger-garlic paste*

1 tsp chopped green chili pepper

½ tsp ground turmeric

⅓ cup chopped mixed red and yellow bell peppers

½ tsp salt

14oz oysters, cleaned and shucked,
  juice reserved

2 tbsp white wine

TO SERVE:

green onion julienne

tomato chutney (page 139)

FOFOS

Goan fish croquettes   GOA, WEST INDIA

Introduced into Goa by the Portuguese, this recipe was originally made with salt cod. I normally use fresh cod or halibut, but you can use any fresh firm fish, or shrimp if you prefer. Ideal party food.

Put the fish into a shallow pan with the fish stock and poach gently for about 10 minutes until just tender. Drain, reserving 3 tbsp stock, and flake the fish, removing any small residual bones. Parboil the potato in salted water for 5–7 minutes, then drain and grate when cool enough to handle.

Put the fish, grated potato, onion, chili pepper, ginger, cumin seeds, and chopped cilantro into a bowl, and mix well. Sprinkle in the cornstarch and stir to mix. Moisten with the reserved fish stock and season with salt and pepper to taste. Add the egg yolk and mix well to combine. Divide the mixture into 16 pieces and shape into croquettes or cylinders.

Heat the oil for deep-frying in a suitable pan to 360°F. Beat the egg white. Dip the fish rolls into the egg white, then deep-fry for 2 minutes or until golden; drain on paper towel. Serve hot, with the tomato chutney.

1lb 2oz cod or halibut fillet

1²/₃ cups fish stock, to poach

1 medium potato, peeled and quartered

salt and freshly ground black pepper

1 red onion, finely chopped

1 green chili pepper, chopped

1 tbsp chopped ginger

1 tsp toasted cumin seeds

1 tbsp chopped cilantro leaves

1½ tbsp cornstarch

1 egg, separated

vegetable oil, to deep-fry

TO SERVE:

tomato chutney (page 139)

VAINGAN KATRI

Stuffed eggplant steaks GUJARAT, WEST INDIA

I have cooked this recipe with different regional influences, but this version from Gujarat is my favorite. Choose medium-sized eggplants – large steaks can be difficult to handle in the pan.

Cut 4 steaks from the widest part of the eggplant, each 3/4-in thick. Scoop out the pulp from the centers, leaving a 3/8-in border intact. Sprinkle lightly with salt and set aside for 30 minutes to disgorge the bitter juices.

Meanwhile, make the stuffing. Cut the potatoes into even-sized pieces and parboil in salted water for 5–7 minutes. Drain and leave until cool enough to handle, then grate finely.

Heat 3 tbsp oil in a sauté pan, wok, or kadhai. Add the asafoetida and, as it sizzles, add the chopped garlic, green chili pepper, and cumin seeds. Sauté for a minute or two until the garlic is light brown in color and the cumin seeds crackle.

Add the grated carrots and cauliflower and sauté for 5 minutes, then stir in the ground coriander, chili powder, and turmeric. Sauté for 30 seconds. Add the grated potatoes, sugar, ginger, and salt, to taste. Cook well for 12–15 minutes, then add the chopped cilantro leaves. Remove from the heat and set aside.

Rinse the eggplant steaks carefully under cold running water and dry with paper towel. Place on a board and spoon the stuffing into the centers. Heat a thin film of oil in a nonstick frying pan. Carefully lift the stuffed eggplant steaks into the pan and fry for about 1 1/2 minutes on each side until golden. Remove and drain on paper towel.

Serve warm, garnished with cilantro sprigs, and accompanied by mustard and yogurt chutney.

14oz eggplant
1/4 tsp salt

STUFFING:
7oz potatoes, peeled
salt
3 tbsp vegetable oil, plus
    extra to shallow-fry
pinch of asafoetida*
1 tsp chopped garlic
1 green chili pepper, chopped
1 tsp cumin seeds
1/2 cup grated carrots
1/2 cup grated cauliflower
2 tsp ground coriander
1/2 tsp Kashmiri red chili powder*
1/2 tsp ground turmeric
1/2 tsp raw sugar or jaggery* (palm sugar)
1 tbsp chopped ginger
3 tbsp chopped cilantro leaves

TO SERVE:
cilantro sprigs, to garnish
mustard and yogurt chutney (page 138)

TANDOORI PANEER AUR HARI GOBI

Roasted paneer and broccoli NORTH INDIA

Barbecues are a year-round event in India, and many Punjabi villages have community tandoori ovens, where locals can take marinated meats or vegetables and bread doughs to cook in the summer evenings or winter afternoons. This recipe is traditionally prepared with cauliflower, but I have used broccoli for color. It works well in a domestic oven, or you can cook it on a barbecue.

First make the roux. Heat the oil in a heavy-based pan, add the gram flour, and cook gently for about 3 minutes, stirring constantly; do not allow to burn. Take off the heat.

Cut the paneer into 1½-in squares, ³/₈-in thick, and place in a shallow dish. Put the ingredients for the paneer marinade into a bowl, add 2 tbsp of the gram flour roux, and whisk together until smooth. Spoon over the paneer, turn to coat, and set aside to marinate in a cool place for 2 hours.

Cut the broccoli into large florets and place in a bowl. Put the ingredients for the broccoli marinade in a blender or mini-processor with 1 tbsp of the gram flour roux and whiz until smooth. Spoon over the broccoli, turn to coat, and set aside in a cool place to marinate for 1 hour.

Preheat oven to 400°F (360°F convection oven). Put the paneer and broccoli in separate roasting trays. Roast in the hot oven for 8–12 minutes until the paneer cubes are golden brown on the surface and the broccoli is tender, basting occasionally with the oil and butter mix.

Arrange the roasted broccoli and paneer on warmed plates, sprinkle with the chaat masala and lime juice, and garnish with salad leaves and apple slices. Serve at once, with the mint chutney.

Note: Paneer is the most popular cheese in India and it is used extensively in cooking. It is a fresh cheese that is drained and pressed into blocks, giving it a firm texture. Paneer is usually cut into cubes or squares and fried, grilled or roasted. It retains its shape well when cooked.

7oz paneer cheese (see note)

9oz broccoli

7 tbsp oil and melted butter mix, to baste

ROUX:

3 tbsp vegetable oil

3 tbsp gram flour*

PANEER MARINADE:

6 tbsp plain yogurt

2 tbsp whipping cream

1 tsp garam masala

1 tsp ground coriander

1 tsp ground turmeric

½ tsp Kashmiri red chili powder*

2 tbsp finely chopped mint leaves

1 tbsp finely chopped ginger

1 tsp toasted cumin seeds, crushed

¼ tsp ground saffron

BROCCOLI MARINADE:

¼ cup garlic cloves, peeled

½ cup (packed) grated Cheddar cheese

4 green chili peppers, roughly chopped

½ tsp salt

7 tbsp whipping cream

TO SERVE:

½ tsp chaat masala*, or to taste

lime juice, to sprinkle

salad leaves and apple slices, to garnish

mint chutney (page 140)

TANDOORI SUBJ CHAAT

Roasted vegetable salad — NORTH INDIA

With a population that is 80% vegetarian, Indian cuisine boasts a wealth of interesting vegetarian dishes. Grilling or roasting vegetables and fruits in a tandoor is common practice in northern India. Here I have used the broiler, but you could cook the skewers on a grill if you prefer. Serve them on the skewers, or rest for a few minutes, then transfer to a bowl and toss with a handful of mixed salad leaves and carrot and mooli (daikon) julienne, as illustrated. Serve with mint chutney (page 140).

First, prepare the marinade. Put all the ingredients into a bowl and mix together thoroughly.

Halve, core, and seed the red peppers, then cut into 1½-in pieces. Cut the star fruit into ⅜-in thick slices. Quarter and core the apples and pear, then cut into 1½-in chunks. Cut the banana into 1½-in chunks.

Add all the fruits and vegetables to the marinade, including the onion. Toss well to mix. If using paneer, cut into 1½-in squares and add to the bowl. Set aside to marinate in a cool place for 30 minutes.

Preheat the broiler to medium-high. Thread the vegetables, fruit, and paneer, if using, alternately onto skewers. Broil, turning occasionally, for 5–7 minutes or until lightly charred.

Serve hot, sprinkled with chaat masala and lime juice.

2 red bell peppers

1 star fruit

1 red apple

1 Granny Smith apple

1 pear

1 banana

1 small red onion, peeled and thinly sliced

3½ oz paneer cheese (optional)

MARINADE:

3 tbsp lime juice, plus extra to sprinkle

1 tbsp toasted cumin seeds, crushed

1 tsp dried chili flakes

1 tbsp chaat masala*, plus extra to sprinkle

1 tsp pomegranate seed powder*

½ tsp salt, or to taste

¾ cup blanched almonds, crushed

⅔ cup plain yogurt

1 tbsp chopped green chili peppers

2 tbsp chopped ginger

3 tbsp vegetable oil

VELLARIKKAI KOSUMALLI

Cucumber salad — TAMIL NADU, SOUTH INDIA

This is a typical south Indian salad – lightly seasoned, highly nutritious, and a perfect cooler in a scorching climate. It is an excellent appetizer and a good accompaniment for most main meals. (Illustrated on page 18)

Halve the cucumber lengthwise and scoop out the seeds, then cut into long julienne strips and place in a bowl. Add the sprouted beans, coconut, chili pepper, chopped cilantro, lemon zest and juice, and salt. Toss the ingredients together to mix and set aside.

Heat the oil in a sauté pan, and add the mustard seeds, black and Bengal gram, asafoetida, dried chili flakes, and curry leaves. Sauté for 1–2 minutes until the spices splutter, then add to the salad and mix well. Serve chilled.

1 large cucumber

2 tbsp mixed sprouted beans

2 tbsp grated fresh coconut*

1 green chili pepper, chopped

2 tbsp chopped cilantro leaves

grated zest and juice of 1 lemon

¼ tsp salt, or to taste

2 tsp vegetable oil

1 tsp mustard seeds

1 tsp each black and Bengal gram*

¼ tsp asafoetida*

½ tsp dried chili flakes

8 curry leaves*

SUNDAL

Chickpea, mango, and coconut salad TAMIL NADU, SOUTH INDIA

Sundal **is a tasty salad and a street food snack, which is particularly popular on the beaches in Chennai. The ingredients are often varied – dried green peas or other beans may replace chickpeas, peanuts are sometimes added, and other fruits may be used instead of mango.**

Drain the chickpeas and put into a saucepan with 1 quart fresh water. Bring to a boil, reduce the heat, and simmer until the chickpeas are cooked, about 2 hours. Season with 1/2 tsp salt after 1 3/4 hours. Drain the chickpeas.

Heat the oil in a sauté pan. Add the mustard seeds and gram, and sauté for a minute or two until the mixture splutters, then add the dried red chili, asafoetida, and curry leaves, and sauté for another minute.

Add the cooked chickpeas and sauté for 2–3 minutes. Remove from the heat. Add the coconut, green chili, mango julienne, chopped plums, if using, and lemon zest and juice. Toss to mix all the salad ingredients together and check the seasoning. Finally, add the chopped cilantro.

Serve warm or cold, garnished with mango slices and cilantro sprigs.

1 1/2 cups chickpeas, soaked in cold water overnight
1/2 tsp salt, or to taste
2 tsp peanut oil
1 tsp mustard seeds
1 tsp black gram*
1 dried red Kashmiri chili pepper*
1/4 tsp asafoetida*
1 tsp chopped curry leaves*
2 tbsp grated fresh coconut*
1 green chili pepper, finely chopped
1/2 green mango, peeled and cut into julienne,
    plus slices to garnish
2 plums, pitted and chopped (optional)
grated zest and juice of 1 lemon
1 tbsp chopped cilantro leaves, plus sprigs
    to garnish

JAL TARANG

Scallop and shrimp salad EAST INDIA

I created this recipe for my restaurant and it is one of my favorites. It is a light, wholesome medley of shellfish, fruit, and salad ingredients with east Indian spicing techniques.

Peel and devein the shrimp; remove the coral (if any) from the scallops. Rinse the shellfish, pat dry, and set aside.

For the dressing, blend all the ingredients together in a blender or food processor until smooth; set aside until needed.

Heat the oil in a sauté pan, add the sesame, nigella, and ajwain seeds and sauté for 2 minutes until they crackle. Add the paprika and ginger, and sauté until the ginger releases its aroma.

Add the shrimp and sauté for 3–4 minutes until they are almost cooked; remove to a bowl and set aside. Add the scallops to the pan and cook for 1 minute until lightly caramelized, then turn them and cook on the other side for 1 minute; remove and add to the shrimp with half of the dressing. Toss to mix and leave for 2 minutes to allow the flavors to be absorbed.

Meanwhile, toss the root vegetable julienne and arugula in about 1 tbsp of the dressing. Arrange the salad and seafood in a large deep plate and sprinkle with the toasted pumpkin and poppy seeds. Pass the rest of the dressing separately.

16 raw large shrimp
12 large scallops, cleaned
4 tsp olive or vegetable oil
1/2 tsp each sesame, nigella*, and ajwain* seeds
1/4 tsp paprika
1 tbsp ginger julienne
handful of mixed carrot, mooli (daikon) and
    beet julienne
handful of wild baby arugula
1 tbsp pumpkin seeds, lightly toasted
1 tbsp mixed black and white poppy seeds, toasted

DRESSING:
1 1/3 cups mixed red and green seedless grapes
3/4 cup mint leaves
2 tbsp roughly chopped ginger
2 small green chili peppers, roughly chopped
1/2 tsp salt, or to taste
1 tsp mango powder* or chaat masala*
4 tsp olive oil or vegetable oil

JHINGA TIL TINKA

Deep-fried shrimp with vermicelli coating NORTH INDIA

These crunchy coated, juicy shrimp are delicious with apple chutney (page 141) as an appetizer. Alternatively, you can serve them as a starter with a light cucumber and tomato salad (page 20), or use to garnish fresh crab salad (as illustrated).

Peel and devein the shrimp, leaving the tail shells intact; wash and pat dry with paper towel. Put all the ingredients for the marinade in a bowl and mix together thoroughly. Add the shrimp, turn to coat, and set aside in a cool place to marinate for 45 minutes.

Mix together the sesame seeds and vermicelli on a plate, for the coating. Remove the shrimp from the marinade and coat liberally with the vermicelli mixture, pressing with your fingers to ensure it adheres. Leave the shrimp to rest for 5 minutes.

Heat the oil for deep-frying in a suitable pan to 360°F. Deep-fry the shrimp, a few at a time, for 2–3 minutes until the coating is golden brown and crunchy. Serve with apple chutney or salad, or use to garnish the crab salad (below).

8 jumbo shrimp
2 tbsp sesame seeds
2oz vermicelli, crumbled
vegetable oil, to deep-fry

MARINADE:
2 garlic cloves, crushed
1/2 tsp Kashmiri red chili powder*
grated zest and juice of 1 lemon
3 tbsp plain yogurt
1 tbsp chopped ginger
1/4 cup grated Cheddar cheese
1 tsp ajwain seeds*
2 tbsp whipping cream
1 tbsp gram flour*, toasted
1/4 tsp green cardamom powder*
1 tsp salt

SALADA DE CARANGUEJOS

Crab salad with coconut and curry leaves GOA, WEST INDIA

All around the Indian coast, there are spectacular shellfish dishes. Preparation and spicing techniques vary with the locality, but curry leaves, fresh coconut, green chilies, and mustard seeds are almost always present. In Goa, this salad is prepared with native blue crabs, but any prepared fresh white crabmeat will do.

Heat the oil in a wok, add the mustard seeds, and sauté until they splutter, then add the curry leaves and sauté for a minute or two. Add the ginger and green chili pepper and cook, stirring, for 2 minutes.

Add the chopped onions and sauté until softened and translucent. Add the crabmeat, stir for a few seconds, then add the turmeric and salt. Sauté for 2 minutes, then stir in the coconut milk, grated coconut, and chopped cilantro. Remove from the heat and allow to cool.

Serve the salad cold, with kumquat or mango and passion fruit chutney.

Variation: For a special presentation (as illustrated), shape the salad neatly using metal rings. Serve each portion topped with a deep-fried coated shrimp (see above) and a sprig of cilantro.

3 tbsp vegetable oil or coconut oil
11/2 tsp mustard seeds
10 curry leaves*, finely chopped
1 tsp finely chopped ginger
1/2 tsp finely chopped green chili pepper
2/3 cup finely chopped onions
10oz white crabmeat, flaked
1 tsp ground turmeric
1/2 tsp salt, or to taste
3 tbsp coconut milk*
1 tbsp grated fresh coconut*
1 tsp chopped cilantro leaves

TO SERVE:
kumquat chutney (page 141), or mango and
    passion fruit chutney (page 140)

FISH AND SHELLFISH

With almost 5000 miles of coastline and warm seas, India is blessed with some of the most exotic fish and seafood in the world. There are fish stalls in almost every coastal village, with huge fish markets in major fishing towns. From Mumbai all around the coast to Calcutta, I have sampled some of the most exquisite fish and shellfish preparations in coastal homes and fishermen's shacks. Traveling around the coast is a real gastronomic experience because preparation and cooking techniques for fish vary so much from one state to another, as you will discover in this chapter.

MEEN MOLEE

Coconut fish curry KERALA, SOUTH INDIA

This recipe from coastal Kerala combines fresh ingredients in a simple way. It is a prime example of Indian minimalist cooking.

Remove any small bones from the fish fillets with tweezers. Mix 1/2 tsp of the salt with 1 tsp of the turmeric and gently rub into the fish fillets.

Heat the coconut oil in a wide pan. Add the onions, chili peppers, and garlic, and sauté for a few minutes, then add the curry leaves and keep cooking until the onion is translucent. Take out half of the curry leaves and set aside for the garnish.

Add the rest of the turmeric and salt to the pan. Pour in the coconut milk and heat through, then add the fish fillets and simmer very gently for 3–4 minutes until just cooked. Serve immediately, garnished with the reserved curry leaves and cilantro.

4 small sea bass fillets, each about 5oz

1 tsp salt, or to taste

1 1/2 tsp ground turmeric

2 tbsp coconut oil or vegetable oil

2 medium onions, finely sliced

6 green chili peppers, slit lengthwise

3 garlic cloves, sliced into fine strips

20 curry leaves*

1 2/3 cups coconut milk*

cilantro sprigs, to garnish

HARI MACHCHI

Fish fried in green spice paste EAST INDIA

I developed this dish while working at the Oberoi hotel in Orissa. I like my flavors to be simple and straightforward and I have always been partial to easy cooking. This recipe is very close to my heart.

Put the fish fillets in a shallow dish, sprinkle with the lemon juice and salt, and leave to marinate for 15 minutes.

Meanwhile, put the ingredients for the green spice paste in a blender or mini-processor and whiz to a fairly smooth paste.

Pat the fish dry with paper towel and coat liberally with the green spice paste, massaging it over the fillets with your fingers. Leave to marinate in the fridge for 40 minutes. In the meantime, wash the spinach, drain well, and cut into julienne. Pat dry thoroughly with paper towel.

Heat the oil in a shallow frying pan. Remove the excess marinade from the fish, then place the fillets flesh-side down in the pan and fry for 2 minutes. Turn the fish over and fry skin-side down for 2–3 minutes or until just cooked.

Meanwhile, heat the oil for deep-frying in a deep-fryer or other deep pan to 360°F and deep-fry the spinach in small batches for 30 seconds or so until crisp. Remove the spinach with a slotted spoon as it stops crackling and drain on paper towel.

When the fish is cooked, remove and drain on paper towel. Serve on warm plates topped with the fried spinach, sprinkled with chaat masala.

4 porgy fillets, each about 5oz

2 tbsp lemon juice

1/2 tsp salt

4 tbsp vegetable oil

GREEN SPICE PASTE:

3/4 cup mint leaves

3/4 cup cilantro leaves

1 1/2 tbsp chopped ginger

2 green chili peppers

1 1/2 tsp dried fenugreek leaf powder*

2 tsp chaat masala*

1 tsp Kashmiri red chili powder*

1/2 tsp salt

2 tbsp gram flour*

DEEP-FRIED SPINACH:

7oz spinach leaves

vegetable oil, to deep-fry

1 tsp chaat masala*

MEEN DAKSHINI

Deccan fish curry ANDHRA PRADESH, SOUTH INDIA

This tangy fish curry has a perfectly balanced combination of south Indian flavors. Red snapper is a good alternative to the *murrel* fish used in Andhra Pradesh. The cuisine of this state is very spicy, but if you have an antidote of a yogurt drink with your meal, you will be fine!

Slice the fish crosswise, through the bone, to give steaks about 1½ in wide; discard the heads if you wish. Mix together the ginger-garlic paste, salt, chili powder, and turmeric. Rub gently into the fish and leave to marinate in the fridge for at least 30 minutes. Meanwhile, soak the tamarind pulp in 1 cup warm water for 20 minutes, then strain through a fine strainer.

    Heat the oil in a frying pan and fry 10 curry leaves until crisp; remove and set aside for the garnish. Add the cumin and mustard seeds to the pan and fry until they begin to crackle. Add the onions and remaining curry leaves, and fry until the onions are softened and golden brown.

    Add the fish and chili peppers, and fry lightly until the peppers have softened, turning once. Add the tamarind liquid and simmer gently for 3–5 minutes until the fish is cooked. Serve sprinkled with the fried curry leaves and chopped cilantro. Accompany with Indian bread or steamed rice.

4 small red snapper or trout, each about 10oz, scaled and cleaned
2 tsp ginger-garlic paste*
½ tsp salt
1 tsp Kashmiri red chili powder*
¼ tsp ground turmeric
1 tbsp tamarind pulp*
3 tbsp sunflower or vegetable oil
20 curry leaves*
1 tsp cumin seeds
½ tsp black mustard seeds
2 medium onions, finely sliced
4 green chili peppers, finely sliced
chopped cilantro leaves, to garnish

DOI MAACH

Spiced fish with yogurt BENGAL, EAST INDIA

Anything *doi* or *jhole* is Bengali, and this recipe epitomises Bengali cuisine. The fish is cooked in yogurt, which curdles as it is heated – a characteristic of this dish. Carp is the traditional choice, but you can use red snapper, cod, sole, porgy, or almost any other fish.

Put the fish fillets in a shallow dish, sprinkle with ¼ tsp of the turmeric, ¼ tsp salt, the ginger-garlic paste, and lemon juice, and leave to marinate in the fridge for about 20 minutes.

    Take out the fish and dust lightly with gram flour. Heat the oil in a shallow frying pan and fry the fillets briefly for about 1 minute each side until golden brown in color. Remove and set aside.

    Add the bay leaf and whole spices to the pan and fry for 1–2 minutes. Add the onion and sauté until it is softened and brown. Add the remaining ¼ tsp turmeric and the chili powder, stir for 20–30 seconds, then add the yogurt, remaining salt, and 7 tbsp water. Bring to a simmer, stirring.

    Add the fried fish pieces and simmer for 3 minutes or until the fish is cooked. Remove from the heat and sprinkle with the Bengali garam masala and chopped cilantro. Serve with boiled rice.

4 red snapper or sole fillets, each about 5oz
½ tsp ground turmeric
½ tsp salt
½ tsp ginger-garlic paste*
½ tsp lemon juice
1 tbsp gram flour*, to dust
2 tbsp vegetable oil
1 bay leaf
½ tsp coriander seeds
1 small dried red Kashmiri chili pepper*
2 cloves
2 green cardamom pods*
2-in piece cassia bark or cinnamon stick
1 medium onion, finely chopped
1 tsp Kashmiri red chili powder*
1¼ cups plain yogurt, lightly whisked
Bengali garam masala*, to sprinkle
1 tsp chopped cilantro leaves

TENGA

Sweet and sour fish curry ASSAM, EAST INDIA

Red snapper steaks make this an Assamese curry with a difference. The original recipe featured *rohu* – a variety of carp found in the river Brahmaputra. Assam produces spices like turmeric, aniseed, and galangal, and its proximity to Myanmar explains the use of Far Eastern ingredients, such as lime leaves, star anise, and bamboo shoots. Here, canned bamboo shoots are used, but fermented bamboo shoot, known as *kharisa*, is more likely to be used in Assam.

Put the fish steaks in a shallow dish. Combine the ingredients for the marinade and rub all over the fish steaks. Set aside in a cool place to marinate for 30 minutes.

Heat the oil in a large frying pan, add the fish steaks, and fry for about 1 minute on each side until lightly colored. Remove the fish to a plate, and set aside.

For the sauce, add the star anise, nigella seeds, and fennel seed to the oil remaining in the pan and sauté for a few minutes until the spices splutter. Add the onions and sauté until softened and golden brown in color.

Add the ground spices and chili powder, sauté for a minute, then add the salt, jaggery, and bamboo shoots. Add the lime leaves, lemon juice, and 1 cup water. Bring to a boil and simmer for a few minutes.

Return the fish steaks to the pan and add the sliced tomato. Cook for 7–8 minutes until the fish is tender, then add the chopped cilantro. Serve garnished with sprigs of cilantro.

Note: Kaffir lime leaves have a highly aromatic lime flavor and are they more typically used in Thai dishes. If unobtainable, substitute the finely grated zest of 1 lime.

4 red snapper steaks, each about 5oz
6 tbsp vegetable oil

MARINADE:
1 tsp finely chopped ginger
½ tsp Kashmiri red chili powder*
½ tsp ground turmeric
1 tsp ground fennel
grated zest and juice of 1 lemon
½ tsp salt
1½ tsp jaggery* (palm sugar)

SAUCE:
1 star anise
1 tsp nigella* or onion seeds
1 tsp fennel seed or aniseed
2 medium onions, finely sliced
1½ tsp ground turmeric
1 tsp Kashmiri red chili powder*
½ tsp ground fennel
½ tsp salt, or to taste
1 tbsp jaggery* (palm sugar)
3½oz bamboo shoots, sliced
3–4 kaffir lime leaves (see note)
2 tbsp lemon juice
1 large tomato, sliced
1 tbsp chopped cilantro, plus extra sprigs to garnish

AMBOT-TIK

Konkani hot and sour fish stew GOA, WEST INDIA

This spicy fish curry can be made with any firm-fleshed fish, such as swordfish, shark, or monkfish. It is a very popular way of serving fish in west India. I like to garnish this dish with green sprouts, but you could use ginger julienne if you prefer.

Cut the swordfish into 1¼-in cubes and set aside. Put the tamarind pulp in a bowl, pour on 7 tbsp warm water, and leave to soak for 20 minutes, then strain through a fine strainer.

Meanwhile, put the ingredients for the chili paste in a blender or mini-processor and whiz to a fairly smooth paste.

Heat the oil in a saucepan, add the onions, and fry gently for about 10 minutes until softened and browned. Add the spice paste and sauté for 5 minutes, then add the tamarind liquid, stirring well. Bring the sauce to a boil and simmer for a minute.

Add the fish cubes and stir to coat in the sauce. Simmer gently for about 5–6 minutes or until just cooked. Check the seasoning, adding salt to taste. Serve garnished with green sprouts and lime slices. Accompany with boiled rice.

1lb swordfish fillet
2 tbsp tamarind pulp*
2 tbsp vegetable oil
1¾ cups finely sliced onions
½ tsp salt, or to taste

CHILI PASTE:
2 tsp vinegar
6 small dried red Kashmiri chili peppers*
6 black peppercorns
1 tsp ground turmeric
1 tbsp ginger-garlic paste*
½ tsp cumin seeds
1 tsp sugar

GARNISH:
green sprouts (eg: broccoli sprouts or curly cress)
lime slices

ISMAILI MACHCHI CURRY

Khoja fish curry WEST INDIA

The Khoja community in India has its own distinctive cuisine, which is quite different from popular Mughlai food. Followers of the Ismaili branch of the Shia sect of Islam, they came to India from Iran, first landing at Gujarat. A strong Gujarati influence is evident in their food, but Khoja dishes maintain their own identity, and they are a real treat. For this recipe, use firm-fleshed fish, like monkfish or angler fish.

Cut the fish into ⅜-in thick slices and place in a shallow dish. Sprinkle with the lemon juice and salt, and leave to marinate for 20 minutes.

Soak the tamarind pulp in 1 cup warm water for 20 minutes, then strain through a fine strainer. Put the ingredients for the coconut spice paste in a blender or mini-processor and whiz to a fine paste.

Heat the oil in a saucepan, add the curry leaves and mustard seeds, and sauté until they crackle. Add the turmeric and coconut spice paste and sauté for 2 minutes or until the fat separates from the paste.

Add the fish and tamarind liquid, and bring to a simmer. Cook over low heat for about 5 minutes until the fish is just cooked. Serve topped with chili peppers and chopped cilantro. Accompany with rice or bread.

1lb monkfish or angler fish fillet
1 tsp lemon juice
½ tsp salt
1 tbsp tamarind pulp*
2 tbsp vegetable oil
10 curry leaves*
1 tsp black mustard seeds
½ tsp ground turmeric

COCONUT SPICE PASTE:
1 cup grated fresh coconut*
10 peppercorns
4 small dried red Kashmiri chili peppers*
6 garlic cloves, peeled

GARNISH:
3 green chili peppers, slit lengthwise
2 tbsp chopped cilantro leaves

NADIR GADH

Fish curry with lotus stems KASHMIR, NORTH INDIA

Kashmiri cooking is unique because the spice pastes, nuts, fruits, and flowers used for flavor, aroma, and color are uncommon in other regions. Here, the flavors are punchy, though the spicing is subtle. Fresh lotus stems are sometimes obtainable from Asian or Chinese grocers, but you can always substitute canned lotus stems. I have used red snapper, but trout works equally well.

Put the fish fillets in a shallow dish, sprinkle with the lemon juice and ½ tsp salt, and leave to marinate for 20 minutes. Meanwhile, whiz the onions in a blender or food processor to a fine paste.

Heat the oil in a frying pan, add the fish fillets, and fry for 1 minute on each side until lightly colored. Remove to a plate, and keep aside.

Add the garlic and sauté for 30 seconds, then add the lotus stems and fry for 2 minutes. Add the chili powder and raw onion paste, and sauté for 3–5 minutes until light brown in color.

Add the cloves, cardamom pods, ginger, turmeric, cassia or cinnamon, salt, and fried onion paste. Pour in 2 cups water, stir well, and bring to a boil. Lower heat and simmer for 10 minutes until the lotus stems are tender.

Add the fish and infused saffron, and simmer gently for 2–3 minutes. Serve sprinkled with toasted cumin seeds and garnished with cilantro.

1lb red snapper fillets, with skin

1 tsp lemon juice

1 tsp salt

1 medium onion, quartered

6 tablespoons vegetable oil

1 tbsp finely chopped garlic

4oz lotus stems, sliced

1 tsp Kashmiri red chili powder*

3 cloves

5 green cardamom pods*

2 black cardamom pods*

1 tsp ground ginger

1½ tsp ground turmeric

1-in piece cassia bark or cinnamon stick

3 tbsp fried onion paste*

pinch of saffron threads, infused in 2 tbsp warm water

½ tsp toasted cumin seeds, crushed

cilantro sprigs, to garnish

NIMBUWALI MACHCHI

Salmon with lime marinade SOUTH INDIA

Cooking fish in a tandoor barbecue is very common in India. This is a popular recipe in the coastal town of Mangalore, where citrus flavors are well liked. It's a great way to spice up salmon.

Cut the salmon into 1½-in large cubes, retaining the skin, and place in a shallow dish.

Put the garlic, cilantro, ginger, lime zest and juice, lime leaves, chili powder, and garam masala in a blender or mini-processor and whiz to a fine paste. Heat the oil in a small pan, add the gram flour, and cook, stirring, for 1–2 minutes to make a roux, without browning.

Mix the roux with the spice paste, salt, and yogurt until smooth. Coat the salmon pieces with the mixture and leave to marinate for 1 hour.

Preheat the oven to 400°F (375°F convection oven), or the broiler to hot. Put the salmon on a rack over a roasting pan and cook for 10–15 minutes, basting once or twice with butter to keep the fish moist.

Serve the salmon hot, accompanied by a seasonal salad.

14oz thick-cut salmon fillet

2 tbsp melted butter, to baste

MARINADE:

20 garlic cloves

small bunch of cilantro, leaves only

1-in piece peeled ginger, lightly crushed

1 tbsp finely grated lime zest

2 tbsp lime juice

4–5 kaffir lime leaves (see note on page 44)

1 tsp Kashmiri red chili powder*

½ tsp garam masala

3 tbsp vegetable oil

1 tbsp gram flour*

½ tsp salt

7 tbsp plain yogurt

MACHER DIYE CHAR DALER KHECHURI

Monkfish kedgeree BENGAL, EAST INDIA

This recipe may look complicated, but in reality it is simple. Kedgeree is one of the culinary imports from India that often appears on our menus. In India, almost every state has its own version. *Elis hilsa* is the local catch used, but any firm-fleshed fish will do; of course, vegetarians can simply leave it out altogether. In eastern India, kedgeree is traditionally served with a range of accompaniments, including pickles, ghee, poppadoms, rice crisps, and yogurt. If preferred the recipe can be simplified by using rice and just one type of lentil, in a 2:1 ratio.

Cut the monkfish into $3/8$-in thick slices. Put half of these into a shallow dish and sprinkle with the lemon juice, chili powder, turmeric, and $1/2$ tsp salt. Turn to coat and set aside in a cool place to marinate for 30 minutes.

Meanwhile, bring 2 cups water to a boil in a shallow pan and add 1 piece of cassia bark or cinnamon stick, 2 of the cloves, 1 of the bay leaves, and $1/2$ tsp of the chopped ginger. Add the other 4 monkfish slices and poach for about 10 minutes until tender, then remove with a slotted spoon and set aside, reserving the poaching liquid.

Put the red lentils, split peas, and Bengal gram in a saucepan with the grated coconut. Add the reserved poaching liquid, $1 1/4$ cups water, and 1 tsp salt. Simmer for about 20–25 minutes until cooked and soft. Drain.

Heat the butter in a separate pan and sauté the remaining cloves, cassia or cinnamon stick, bay leaves, ginger, cumin seeds, and dried red chili peppers for 1 minute. Add the rice and mung beans or green lentils. Stir, then add 1 tsp salt, the sugar, and $1 2/3$ cups water to cover the mixture. Bring to a boil, then lower the heat, and simmer for about 20 minutes until the rice and lentils are cooked and all the liquid is absorbed. Meanwhile, flake the poached monkfish with a fork.

In a separate pan, heat the oil and fry the marinated pieces of fish for about 6–8 minutes until crisp and golden brown on the surface, and cooked through to the center.

With a fork, mix together the rice, boiled lentils, poached monkfish, and chopped cilantro. Serve the kedgeree hot, topped with the fried monkfish pieces, cilantro sprigs, and a spoonful of cilantro and peanut chutney.

Cilantro and peanut chutney: Whiz $1 1/2$ cups cilantro leaves, $3/4$ cup mint leaves, $1/4$ cup toasted peanuts, $1 1/2$ tbsp chopped ginger, 1 green chili pepper, 2 tbsp lemon juice, 1 tsp salt, and 1 tbsp water together in a blender or mini-processor to make a paste. Correct the seasoning.

7oz monkfish or angler fish fillet

1 tsp lemon juice

$1/2$ tsp Kashmiri red chili powder*

$1/2$ tsp ground turmeric

salt

2 x 1-in pieces cassia bark or cinnamon sticks

6 cloves

3 bay leaves

2 tbsp chopped ginger

$2 1/2$ tbsp dried split red lentils

$2 1/2$ tbsp dried split peas

$2 1/2$ tbsp dried split Bengal gram*

$3/4$ cup (rounded) grated fresh coconut*

2 tbsp butter

1 tsp cumin seeds

2 small dried red Kashmiri chili peppers*

$1 1/2$ cups short-grain risotto rice

$2 1/2$ tbsp mung beans or green lentils

$1/2$ tsp sugar

$1 1/2$ tbsp vegetable oil

1 tbsp chopped cilantro leaves

cilantro sprigs, to garnish

TO SERVE:

cilantro and peanut chutney (see left)

SANDHNO NO PATIO

Jumbo shrimp curry GUJARAT, WEST INDIA

This recipe takes its name from the pan or *patio* it is cooked in. The best shrimp *patio* recipe comes from Bharuch, an old Parsi town on the banks of the River Narmada. This unique town was the first hold of the Parsi community in India and boasts an 800-year-old fire temple. Parsi cuisine is a good blend of Iranian and Indian ingredients. If you cannot find fresh fenugreek leaves for this recipe, use chopped spinach leaves instead.

Peel and devein the shrimp, leaving the tails attached. Rinse and pat dry. Next prepare the green spice paste. Put all the ingredients in a blender or mini-processor and whiz to a fine paste. Spread half of the paste all over the shrimp and set aside to marinate for 30 minutes.

Heat half of the vegetable and sesame seed oils in a *patio* or deep sauté pan. Add the remaining spice paste and sauté gently for 2 minutes. Add the chopped onions and salt, and sauté until translucent, then add the rest of the ingredients except the shrimp.

Heat the remaining oil in a separate sauté pan and fry the marinated shrimp for 1–2 minutes. Add the shrimp to the onion mixture and simmer for about 5 minutes until they are cooked. Serve at once.

8–12 jumbo raw shrimp

2 tbsp vegetable oil

1 tbsp sesame seed oil

2 large onions, finely chopped

½ tsp salt

2 tsp chopped garlic

1 tsp ground turmeric

2 bunches of fenugreek leaves, stems removed

1 tbsp dried fenugreek leaves

2 tbsp cilantro leaves

1 bunch of green onions, trimmed and sliced

GREEN SPICE PASTE:

3 green chili peppers

¾ cup cilantro leaves and stems

1 tsp ground turmeric

3 dried red Kashmiri chili peppers*, seeded

1 tsp cumin seeds

1 tsp black peppercorns

ROYYALU PULUSU

Shrimp curry ANDHRA PRADESH, SOUTH INDIA

I once thought that everything from southern India came from Madras. When I was sent south for my education, I was amazed at the colors, architecture, cuisine, religion, and culture. It was so varied and different from the robust north. I picked up this recipe from a friend's mother in the coastal town of Kakinada.

Peel and devein the shrimp, leaving the tails attached. Rinse and pat dry. Mix together the mango powder, turmeric, chili powder, and salt, then rub over the shrimp and leave to marinate in a cool place for 20 minutes or so.

Heat the oil in a sauté pan and sauté the onions until softened and golden. Add the ginger-garlic paste and cook well for 2–3 minutes.

Add the ground coriander, cumin, grated coconut, green chili peppers, peppercorns, mint, and curry leaves, and sauté gently for 2–3 minutes.

Add the shrimp and sauté for 1 minute. Pour in the coconut milk and simmer for 5 minutes, then add the chopped tomatoes and 7 tbsp water. Simmer over a low heat for 4–5 minutes until the shrimp are just cooked.

Scatter with chopped cilantro and serve with chapattis or boiled rice.

10oz medium raw shrimp (about 16)

½ tsp mango powder*

¼ tsp ground turmeric

¼ tsp Kashmiri red chili powder*

½ tsp salt

¼ cup sesame seed oil

4 medium onions, sliced

2 tsp ginger-garlic paste*

1 tsp each ground coriander and cumin

1¼ cups grated fresh coconut*

2 green chili peppers, chopped

½ tsp crushed peppercorns

1 tbsp chopped mint leaves

1 tsp chopped curry leaves*

1 cup coconut milk*

2 tomatoes, chopped

2 tbsp chopped cilantro leaves

CHEMEEN MANGA CHARU

Shrimp and green mango curry KERALA, SOUTH INDIA

This dish comes from the Moplah Muslims of Kerala, a community descended from 7th century Arabs. Its fragrant mix of coconut, curry leaves, and fresh seafood is typical of Kerala.

Peel and devein the shrimp, leaving the tail attached. Rinse and pat dry.

Heat 1 tbsp of the coconut oil in a sauté pan, add the coconut, chopped onion and fennel seeds, and sauté over a medium heat until the coconut is golden brown. Remove and grind to a smooth paste, using a blender.

Heat 2 tbsp of the coconut oil in the pan. Add the sliced onion and fry until translucent. Add the green chili peppers with the ginger-garlic paste, and sauté for 2–3 minutes. Stir in the ground spices and half the mango strips.

Add the shrimp to the pan with the salt and cook, stirring, until they are opaque and almost cooked. Stir in the coconut paste, coconut milk, and the rest of the mango. Simmer gently until the shrimp are just cooked.

Meanwhile, heat the remaining 1 tbsp coconut oil in a separate pan and sauté the fenugreek seeds, mustard seeds, and curry leaves until aromatic. Serve the shrimp curry topped with the aromatic spice mixture and green mango strips. Accompany with rice or Indian bread.

10oz large raw shrimp (about 16)
4 tbsp coconut oil or vegetable oil
3/4 cup grated fresh coconut*
1/2 onion, finely chopped
1 tsp fennel seeds
1 onion, finely sliced
2 green chili peppers, chopped
1 1/2 tsp garlic-ginger paste*
1 1/2 tsp ground coriander
1 tsp Kashmiri red chili powder*
1/2 tsp ground turmeric
3 1/2 oz green mango, sliced into thin strips, plus extra to garnish
1/2 tsp salt, or to taste
1 cup coconut milk*
1 tsp fenugreek seeds
1 tsp black mustard seeds
25 curry leaves*

MOCHHA CHINGRI MAACHHER MOLAI CURRY

Lobster curry with coconut BENGAL, EAST INDIA

Everything is dramatic in Bengal, including this preparation with its impeccable spicing and flavoring. Rock or deep-sea lobster would be used in this part of India, but consider any lobster suitable.

Split the lobsters in two lengthwise, clean, and smear with the turmeric and 1/2 tsp salt. Process the onions in a blender or food processor to a paste.

Heat the oil in a deep sauté pan. Add the lobsters and sauté lightly for 2 minutes or until the shells color; remove and set aside. Add the potatoes to the pan and sauté for a few minutes until golden. Remove and set aside.

Heat the ghee or butter in a saucepan and sauté the bay leaves, cloves, cassia or cinnamon, and cardamom pods for 1–2 minutes. Add the onion paste and cook for 3–4 minutes until lightly cooked. Add the chili and ginger-garlic pastes and sauté for a further 2 minutes until the masala is well cooked, adding a little water from time to time to keep it moist.

Add the potato with the sugar and remaining 1/2 tsp salt. Pour in half the coconut milk and bring to a simmer. Add the lobster and simmer for 10 minutes. Add the rest of the coconut milk and simmer for a further 5–10 minutes until the lobster and potatoes are cooked. Serve with rice.

2 medium raw lobsters, each about 14oz
2 tsp ground turmeric
1 tsp salt
1 cup roughly chopped onions
4 tbsp vegetable or coconut oil
1 medium potato, peeled and cut into wedges
1 tbsp ghee* or butter
2 bay leaves
2 cloves
2-inch piece cassia bark or cinnamon stick
2 green cardamom pods*
2 tsp green chili paste*
1 1/2 tsp ginger-garlic paste*
1 tsp sugar
1 2/3 cups coconut milk*

CARIL DE CARANGUEJOS

Goan crab curry — WEST INDIA

Choosing good crabs for this recipe is critical – select those that are very fresh and feel heavy for their size, rather than the largest ones. If possible, buy live crabs and get your fishmonger to cut them up for you close to the time you want to cook. I use raw crab to ensure all the juices are retained in the sauce, but you can use cooked crab.

Cut each crab into 4 or 5 pieces (unless your fishmonger has done so for you). Make sure the small stomach sac behind the mouth and the inedible gray feathery gills are removed.

Soak the tamarind pulp in 1 cup warm water for 20 minutes, then strain through a fine strainer. Mix together the ginger-garlic paste, chili powder, cumin, and coriander with 3 tbsp water to make a paste.

Heat the oil in a large sauté pan and sauté the onions until softened and light brown. Add the spice paste and sauté gently for 3–4 minutes.

Add the tamarind liquid and salt. Bring to a simmer, add the crabs, and simmer for about 5 minutes until almost cooked. Add the coconut milk, check the seasoning, and simmer for a further 3–4 minutes until the crab is cooked. Serve with rice.

2 medium crabs (preferably raw), each about 1lb 2oz
2½ tbsp tamarind pulp*
2 tsp ginger-garlic paste*
1½ tsp Kashmiri red chili powder*
1 tsp ground cumin
½ tsp ground coriander
3 tbsp vegetable oil
1⅓ cups thinly sliced onions
½ tsp salt, or to taste
7 tbsp coconut milk*

GARNISH:
chopped cilantro leaves
crushed pepper

EGURU PETHELU

Crab with tamarind and curry leaves — ANDHRA PRADESH, SOUTH INDIA

Curried crabs are a regular feature in the coastal towns of Andhra Pradesh. I first tasted this recipe in a friend's house in Kakinada – his Telangana fisherman cook made it for us. Experiencing the intense sweet flavors of seafood with simple spicing was unforgettable.

Cut each crab into 4 or 5 pieces (or ask your fishmonger to). Remove the stomach sac and gills. Crack the claws and set aside. Soak the tamarind pulp in ⅔ cup warm water for 20 minutes; strain through a fine strainer.

Heat the oil in a sauté pan, add the dried chili peppers, and sauté for a minute or two, then remove. Add the curry leaves to the pan and sauté until they crackle. Add the onions and fry until softened and light brown.

Add the ginger-garlic paste and sauté for 3–4 minutes until it turns golden brown and the raw taste disappears. Add the coconut paste and fry for a few minutes until the oil separates. Add the ground coriander and turmeric, and sauté over a low heat for 1 minute.

Add the crabs, salt, and tamarind liquid. Simmer gently for 5–8 minutes, or until the crab pieces are cooked, then take them out. Boil the sauce to reduce slightly. Return the crab and scatter with cilantro to serve.

2 medium crabs (preferably raw), each about 1lb 2oz
2½ tbsp tamarind pulp*
¼ cup vegetable oil
2 dried red Kashmiri chili peppers*
8–10 curry leaves*
2⅔ cups thinly sliced onions
2 tsp ginger-garlic paste*
⅔ cup coconut paste* or creamed coconut
2 tsp ground coriander
¾ tsp ground turmeric
½ tsp salt, or to taste
2 tbsp chopped cilantro leaves

POULTRY AND GAME

Chicken has a prime place in Indian cooking. I have always maintained that chickens in India taste like the real thing, unlike the majority in this country, which have been fast-bred in restrictive cages. In India, chickens exercise well and that helps to develop flavor. Before cooking, poultry is skinned and cut into pieces to encourage spicy flavors to penetrate the flesh. Game is popular in India, though it is now more limited than it used to be, owing to hunting restrictions. Geese, pigeon, partridge, and quail feature on luxurious Indian tables, alongside chicken and duck.

CHUTNEY NI MURGI

Chicken cooked in tangy herb paste GUJARAT, WEST INDIA

Cooking with conflicting flavors is an art, but mixing flavors, textures, and colors is something that is natural to Parsi people. I have sampled this dish many times – my friend Chef Cyrus Todiwala cooks it to perfection.

First make the chutney. Whiz all the ingredients together in a blender with 2–3 tbsp water to make a smooth paste. Keep in the fridge until required.

Cut the chicken into 2-in cubes. Heat half the oil in a large deep sauté pan, add the onion, and sauté until softened and golden. Stir in the ginger-garlic paste and sauté for 1 minute, then add the chicken. Sauté until the chicken is lightly browned, then add 1/2 cup water, bring to a boil, and simmer for 10 minutes.

Heat the rest of the oil in a separate pan, add the chutney, and stir-fry until the oil separates from the chutney. Add the chicken, together with its juices, and the salt. Simmer for about 15 minutes until the chicken is cooked and the sauce has reduced to a coating consistency. Stir in the lemon juice, and serve garnished with ginger and shredded mint.

1 lb 2 oz skinless, boneless chicken thighs or breasts
6 tbsp sunflower oil
1 large onion, finely chopped
2 tsp ginger-garlic paste*
1/2 tsp salt
3 tbsp lemon juice

CHUTNEY:
3 1/2 oz green mango, grated
large bunch of cilantro, chopped
small bunch of mint, chopped
8 garlic cloves, sliced
1 tbsp chopped ginger
1 1/4 cups grated fresh coconut*

GARNISH:
ginger julienne and shredded mint

CARIL DE GALINHA

Goan chicken curry GOA, WEST INDIA

As is the case in any country, every household will have its own favorite recipe for a particular dish. Chicken curry recipes are innumerable in India. Here is the Goan version – simple with straightforward bold flavors.

Cut the chicken into 8 pieces and remove the skin. Soak the tamarind pulp in 7 tbsp warm water for 20 minutes, then strain through a fine strainer.

For the coconut spice paste, put the garlic, ginger, chilies, and dry ingredients in a blender or mini-processor and process until finely ground. Add the 7 tbsp coconut milk and whiz to a fairly smooth paste.

Heat the oil in a large deep sauté pan. Add the onions and sauté until softened and golden brown in color. Stir in the coconut spice paste and sauté over a medium heat for 3–5 minutes.

Add the chicken pieces to the pan and sauté until they are lightly colored. Add the salt and half the coconut milk, then simmer for about 15–20 minutes until the chicken is almost cooked. Add the tamarind liquid and remaining coconut milk. Bring to a simmer and cook for a further 5 minutes or so until the chicken is done. Sprinkle with chopped cilantro and serve with boiled rice.

2 3/4 lb whole chicken
3 tbsp tamarind pulp*
3 tbsp vegetable oil
2 onions, sliced
1/2 tsp salt, or to taste
1 2/3 cups coconut milk*
1 tbsp chopped cilantro leaves

COCONUT SPICE PASTE:
6–8 garlic cloves, peeled
1-in piece peeled ginger
4 green chili peppers
4 small dried red Kashmiri chili peppers*
1 tbsp rice flour or ground rice
1 tsp coriander seeds
1 tbsp poppy seeds
1 tbsp ground turmeric
1 tsp ground cumin
7 tbsp coconut milk*

PALOK DIYE TIKHA MURGI KALIA

Spicy chicken curry with spinach BENGAL, EAST INDIA

This recipe reflects the merging of cooking styles. Here it is the Muslim influence on Bengali cooking. The word _kalia_ means a dark color sauce in Muslim Indian cooking, so this Bengali recipe has undergone some changes in spicing and cooking technique. To me, Calcutta has always been a great inspiration for cooking. I have found terrific dishes with Muslim characteristics, and I dream of returning with plenty of time on hand to explore English, Jewish, and Chinese influences on the local cuisine.

Cut the chicken into 8 pieces and remove the skin. Heat the oil in a deep sauté pan to smoking point, then remove from the heat, and let cool slightly. Return to a medium heat, add the dried chili peppers, whole spices, and bay leaf, and sauté until the spices crackle.

Add the onions and fry until softened and light brown in color. Add the ginger-garlic paste and cook well for 2–3 minutes to lose the raw flavor.

Add the chicken pieces and sauté to seal on all sides. Add the chili powder, coriander, and turmeric, and sauté for 1 minute. Stir in the chopped tomatoes, salt, and 7 tbsp water. Bring to a simmer and cook gently for about 20 minutes until the chicken is done.

Meanwhile, cook the spinach. Heat the mustard oil in a separate pan and sauté the crushed red chili and chopped garlic for a few minutes until the garlic turns light brown. Stir in the turmeric and salt, and sauté for 30 seconds. Add the spinach leaves and sauté until they have just wilted.

Add the wilted spinach to the chicken curry and simmer for 3–5 minutes to allow the flavors to blend together. Remove from the heat and sprinkle with the garam masala and chopped gingèr. Serve in bowls, accompanied by steamed rice.

2¾ lb whole chicken

¼ cup mustard oil or vegetable oil

2 dried red Kashmiri chili peppers*

3 cloves

3 black cardamom pods*

1-in piece cassia bark or cinnamon stick

1 bay leaf

2½ cups sliced onions

1½ tsp ginger-garlic paste*

1 tsp Kashmiri red chili powder*

1 tsp ground coriander

1 tsp ground turmeric

1 cup chopped fresh tomatoes

½ tsp salt, or to taste

SPINACH:

2 tbsp mustard oil or vegetable oil

1 dried red Kashmiri chili pepper*, finely crushed

1 tsp chopped garlic

½ tsp ground turmeric

½ tsp salt

1¼ lb spinach leaves, trimmed and chopped

TO SERVE:

1 tsp Bengali garam masala*

2 tsp finely chopped ginger

HYDERABADI KALI MIRICH KA MURG

Peppery chicken curry HYDERABAD, SOUTH INDIA

Black pepper is a favored spice in Hyderabad. This recipe brings the full flavor of freshly crushed pepper into the sauce rather than drawing on its fiery heat. The final sprinkling of toasted pepper makes a huge difference.

Joint the chicken into 8 pieces and put into a shallow dish. Mix together the ginger-garlic paste, salt, vinegar, turmeric, and 1 tsp crushed peppercorns. Spread over the chicken, cover, and marinate in the fridge for 2–3 hours.

Put the chopped large onions into a blender or food processor and process to a paste; set aside.

Heat the oil in a large deep sauté pan, add the remaining 2 tsp crushed peppercorns, and sauté for 1 minute, then add the sliced onions. Cook gently until softened and golden. Next add the onion paste and fry gently for about 20 minutes until golden brown in color.

Add the chicken with the marinade and sauté until the liquid evaporates. Add about 1 cup water, bring to a simmer, and cook for about 20 minutes until the chicken is done. Serve sprinkled with ginger julienne, green sprouts, and toasted crushed pepper. Accompany with Indian breads.

2³/4 lb whole chicken
2 tsp ginger-garlic paste*
1/2 tsp salt, or to taste
2 tbsp white vinegar or lemon juice
1 tsp ground turmeric
3 tsp black peppercorns, freshly crushed
2 large onions, roughly chopped
7 tbsp vegetable oil
2 medium onions, sliced

GARNISH:
ginger julienne
green sprouts (eg: broccoli or mustard sprouts, or curly cress)
1 tsp crushed peppercorns, lightly toasted

KOZHI VARTHA KOZHAMBU

Chettinad chicken curry TAMIL NADU, SOUTH INDIA

I must have tasted countless versions of this recipe while training as a chef in south India. I acquired this particular recipe while working in the Taj Connemara hotel from a line cook, whom we called *Thambi*, meaning younger brother. I have no idea what his real name was, but his grasp of Tamilian cooking was amazing and I learned so many techniques from him.

Cut the chicken into 8 pieces and remove the skin. To make the spice paste, put all the ingredients in a blender or mini-processor with 3 tbsp water and whiz to a fine paste.

Heat the oil in a large deep sauté pan, add the onions, and sauté until softened and light brown. Add the curry leaves and spice paste, and sauté for 2–3 minutes, then stir in the chili powder, coriander, and turmeric and cook, stirring, for 30 seconds.

Add the chicken pieces and sauté for a few minutes until golden. Add the coconut milk, salt, and chopped tomatoes, and bring to a simmer. Continue to simmer for 20 minutes or until the chicken is cooked. Sprinkle with the chopped cilantro leaves to serve.

2³/4 lb whole chicken
4¹/2 tbsp coconut oil or vegetable oil
1²/3 cups sliced onions
20 curry leaves*
1 tsp Kashmiri red chili powder*
1 tsp each ground coriander and turmeric
1²/3 cups coconut milk*
1/2 tsp salt, or to taste
1/3 cup chopped tomatoes
2 tbsp chopped cilantro leaves

SPICE PASTE:
1 tbsp peeled, chopped ginger
2 tbsp chopped garlic
3 cloves
10 black peppercorns
1¹/2 tsp fennel seeds
1-in piece cassia bark or cinnamon stick

KOZHI VELLAI KAZHAMBU

White chicken curry TAMIL NADU, SOUTH INDIA

This is one of the mild chicken curries of Tamil Nadu and I strongly recommend it – the flavors are unbelievable. Don't be put off by the lengthy ingredients list – everything is available from good grocery stores and supermarkets. In the original recipe, shelled *mocjakka* beans are used. I have substituted fava beans, but you can use limas, or omit them altogether if you prefer.

Cut the chicken into strips, about 1 in wide, and place in a shallow dish.

To make the spice paste, heat the oil in a deep sauté pan and add the onion, ginger, garlic, spices, and cashew nuts. Sauté lightly until the onions are softened, without coloring them. Allow to cool, then whiz to paste with the yogurt, using a blender or mini-processor.

Coat the chicken with the spice paste, cover, and leave to marinate in a cool place for about 30 minutes.

For the seasoning, heat the oil in the clean sauté pan. Add the bay leaf and whole spices, and sauté for a minute or two. Add the onions and fry gently until they are softened and translucent.

Add the fava beans and coated chicken strips to the pan, and sauté lightly for 3–5 minutes. Add the coconut milk and ginger julienne, and bring to a simmer. Continue to simmer gently for 12–15 minutes or until the chicken is cooked. Remove from the heat and add the chopped cilantro leaves, lime zest and juice.

Serve the curry in bowls, garnished with cilantro sprigs and lime slices. Accompany with rice.

Note: If you are able to obtain very young fava beans, use them whole in the pod, slicing diagonally into 1-in pieces.

1¼ lb skinless, boneless chicken breasts
⅔ cup podded fava beans
1¾ cups coconut milk*
1½-in piece ginger, peeled and julienned

SPICE PASTE:
2 tsp vegetable oil
1 large onion, sliced
2 tbsp chopped ginger
10 garlic cloves, chopped
1-in piece cassia bark or cinnamon stick
2 cloves
2 green cardamom pods*
1 tsp fennel seeds
8 green chili peppers
1 tsp coriander seeds
¼ cup cashew nuts
7 tbsp plain yogurt

SEASONING:
2 tbsp vegetable oil
1 bay leaf
1 star anise
2 cloves
1-in piece cassia bark or cinnamon stick
2 onions, sliced

TO FINISH:
2 tbsp chopped cilantro leaves
grated zest and juice of 1 lime
cilantro sprigs and lime slices, to garnish

METHI KUKKUR

Chicken cooked in fenugreek leaves — NORTH INDIA

Among the various greens I was forced to eat by my parents in childhood, fenugreek is something I have always enjoyed immensely. It is a versatile ingredient in Indian cooking – used as a herb, green, spice, medicine, marinade, and flavor enhancer. Dried powdered fenugreek leaves give this recipe its characteristic flavor; if you are unable to obtain fresh fenugreek leaves for the garnish, simply omit. Use chicken thighs rather than a whole chicken if you prefer.

Cut the chicken into 8 pieces, then remove the skin and put the pieces into a shallow dish. Mix the yogurt with 1 tsp salt and the green chili paste. Spread all over the chicken, then cover and leave to marinate in a cool place for 45 minutes.

Heat the oil in a large deep sauté pan. Add the cardamom pods, cloves, and cassia or cinnamon, and sauté until the spices crackle. Add the sliced onions and sauté until softened and light brown in color.

Add the ginger-garlic paste and cook well for 3–4 minutes to lose the raw aromas. Stir in the chili powder, turmeric, and coriander, and sauté for 1 minute. Add the chopped tomatoes and simmer for about 10 minutes until they are soft and the fat separates from the sauce.

Add the chicken pieces with the marinade and cook over a low heat for 15–20 minutes until the chicken is tender.

Meanwhile, prepare the garnish. Rinse the fenugreek leaves, drain well, and pat dry with paper towel. Heat the oil for deep-frying in a deep-fryer or other deep pan to 360°F, and deep-fry the fenugreek for 20–30 seconds or so until crisp. Remove with a slotted spoon as it stops crackling and drain on paper towel.

Add the fenugreek leaf powder, chopped ginger, and cilantro to the chicken, and check the seasoning. Serve topped with the deep-fried fenugreek, and accompanied by Indian breads.

2³⁄₄ lb whole chicken
³⁄₄ cup plain yogurt
1 tsp salt, or to taste
2 tsp green chili paste*
5 tbsp vegetable oil
6 green cardamom pods*
1 black cardamom pod*
3 cloves
1-in piece cassia bark or cinnamon stick
2¹⁄₂ cups thinly sliced onions
2 tbsp ginger-garlic paste*
1 tsp Kashmiri red chili powder*
1 tsp ground turmeric
1 tsp ground coriander
³⁄₄ cup chopped fresh tomatoes
1 tbsp dried fenugreek leaf powder*
1 tbsp finely chopped ginger
2 tbsp chopped cilantro leaves

GARNISH:
large handful of fresh fenugreek leaves
oil, to deep-fry

TANDOORI MURG

Tandoori spice roasted chicken NORTH INDIA

This famous dish is universally popular. Traditionally roasted in a tandoor in Indian kitchens, it is a simple recipe that can be cooked easily in a domestic oven or on the grill.

Cut the chicken into 4 pieces (2 leg quarters and 2 breasts with wing bones attached). Make 3 or 4 deep incisions in each piece without cutting right through the flesh, then place in a shallow dish. Mix the lemon juice with the ginger-garlic paste, salt, and chili powder. Spread all over the chicken and set aside for 20 minutes to allow the juices to drain.

Meanwhile, mix together the ingredients for the spiced yogurt marinade. Drain the chicken, coat with the spiced yogurt mixture, and set aside to marinate for 2 hours.

Preheat the oven to 400°F (360°F convection oven). Put the chicken on a rack resting in a roasting pan and roast for 12–15 minutes. Take out of the oven and baste with the butter and oil mixture. Return the chicken to the oven and cook for a further 3–5 minutes or until it is cooked. Remove and rest on the rack for 5 minutes or so.

Serve the chicken sprinkled with lime juice and chaat masala, and accompanied with a salad and mint chutney (page 140).

2¼ lb whole chicken
oil and melted butter, to baste
2 tbsp lemon juice
1 tbsp ginger-garlic paste*
1 tsp salt
1 tsp Kashmiri red chili powder*

SPICED YOGURT MARINADE:
1 cup thick yogurt
1 tsp garam masala
7 tbsp vegetable oil
½ tsp ground cinnamon
½ tsp Kashmiri red chili powder*
1 tsp salt
pinch of edible red food coloring (optional)

TO SERVE:
1½ tsp lime juice
1 tsp chaat masala*

ACHARI MURG

Rajasthani pickled chicken curry RAJASTHAN, NORTH INDIA

Rajasthan is a dry desert state and local people like to cook with a lot of oil to add succulence and preserve the food for longer. This curry has been popular in my restaurant for some time. It is a no-fuss recipe and a good meal can be built around it. The listed whole spices can be replaced with a spice mix called panch phoran* if you like.

Cut the chicken thighs in half and set aside. Heat the oil in a large deep sauté pan and add the whole spices and garlic cloves. Sauté until the spices crackle and the garlic turns light brown in color, then add the whole red chili peppers and sauté for 30 seconds.

Add the sliced onions and sauté until softened and light brown in color, then add the ginger-garlic paste and cook for 2–3 minutes. Stir in the tomato paste and 7 tbsp water, and bring to a simmer.

Add the chicken to the pan and simmer for 15 minutes. Stir in the jaggery or raw sugar if using, lemon juice, and salt. Stir in the yogurt and simmer gently for a further 5 minutes; do not boil. Check the seasoning and serve sprinkled with cilantro leaves.

1 lb 2oz skinless, boneless chicken thighs
7 tbsp vegetable oil
¼ tsp black mustard seeds
¼ tsp cumin seeds
¼ tsp fennel seeds
¼ tsp fenugreek seeds
¼ tsp onion seeds
10 peeled garlic cloves
5 small red chili peppers
1¼ cups thinly sliced onions
1 tbsp ginger-garlic paste*
2 tbsp tomato paste
1½ tbsp jaggery* or raw sugar (optional)
2 tbsp lemon juice
1 tsp salt, or to taste
¾ cup plain yogurt, lightly whisked
2 tbsp chopped cilantro leaves

MURG TARIWALA

Home-style chicken curry NORTH INDIA

You can't go wrong cooking this simple curry, unless you leave the pot on the stove and leave for a long vacation! It is best prepared with free-range chicken on the bone, but if you buy boneless chicken, I recommend chicken thighs.

Cut the chicken into large pieces. Pound all the whole spices together using a mortar and pestle, spice grinder, or mini-processor.

Heat the oil in a saucepan. Add the spice mix and bay leaf, and sauté for a minute or two until the mixture crackles. Add the sliced onions and sauté until softened and golden brown.

Add the ginger-garlic paste, and cook gently, stirring continuously, for 2–3 minutes – keep scraping the bottom of the pan to prevent the mixture sticking and burning. Stir in the chili powder, coriander, and turmeric and cook briefly, stirring constantly.

Add the chopped tomatoes, tomato paste, and salt. Cook over a low heat, stirring occasionally. As the tomatoes break down to form a sauce, add the chicken. Bring to a simmer and cook gently for about 20 minutes.

When the chicken is almost cooked, sprinkle with the garam masala, and simmer for a little longer to finish cooking. Add the chopped cilantro leaves and chopped ginger, then serve.

1¼ lb chicken thighs or breasts, skinned
6 green cardamom pods*
1-in piece cassia bark or cinnamon stick
1 tsp black peppercorns
1 star anise
2 tsp cumin seeds
4 cloves
7 tbsp vegetable oil
1 bay leaf
2 cups finely sliced onions
1 tbsp ginger-garlic paste*
1½ tsp Kashmiri red chili powder*
1½ tsp ground coriander
1½ tsp ground turmeric
⅓ cup roughly chopped tomatoes
1 tbsp tomato paste
1 tsp salt, or to taste
1 tsp garam masala
2 tbsp chopped cilantro leaves
1 tbsp finely chopped ginger

MURG HARA MASALA

Herb flavored chicken WEST INDIA

Green chicken curries are numerous in India and every region has its own. I picked up this simple, exquisite recipe from my Khoja friends in Mumbai. The Khoja Muslim community has a unique way of preparing and cooking food, which lends distinctive flavors.

Cut the chicken into 1-in dice. Soak the tamarind pulp in 1 cup warm water for 20 minutes, then strain through a fine strainer.

To prepare the spice paste, soak the nuts in warm water to cover for 10 minutes; drain. Sauté the garlic cloves in oil until golden; cool. Put all the spice paste ingredients in a blender or mini-processor and whiz to a paste.

Heat the oil in a deep sauté pan and sauté the chopped ginger and green chili peppers for 2–3 minutes until softened. Add the spice paste and sauté lightly for a minute or two. Add the tamarind liquid and salt, and bring to a simmer.

Add the chicken to the sauce and simmer for about 15–20 minutes until the chicken is cooked. Serve with rice or Indian breads.

1¼ lb skinless, boneless chicken thighs or breasts
4 tbsp tamarind pulp*
4½ tbsp vegetable oil
1 tbsp finely chopped ginger
1½ tsp finely chopped green chili pepper
1 tsp salt, or to taste

SPICE PASTE:
⅔ cup cashew nuts
⅓ cup garlic cloves, peeled
oil, to fry
1¼ cups fried onion paste*
2½ cups cilantro leaves
2½ cups mint leaves
10 green chili peppers
¼ cup peeled, sliced ginger

NAADAN KOZHI ULARTHIYATHU

Kochi chicken curry KERALA, SOUTH INDIA

Kerala is divided geographically into three areas by its communities – north is home to the Muslims, Syrian Christians and Jews live in the center, while the south is inhabited by Hindus. Not surprisingly, there are strong regional and cultural influences on Keralan cuisine. Every time I visit Kochi, formerly Cochin, I eat at a tiny restaurant called Naadan – literally a cooking pot. It is where I first tasted this fragrant curry, which works equally well with duck, pigeon, and rabbit.

Cut the chicken into 8 pieces and remove the skin.

To make the spice powder, grind all the spices together, using a spice grinder, mini-processor, or mortar and pestle.

Heat the oil in a deep sauté pan. Add the sliced onions and sauté until softened and light brown in color. Add the ginger and garlic, and cook, stirring, for 2–3 minutes to lose the raw aromas. Add the green chilies and sauté for 1 minute. Stir in the spice powder and salt, and cook, stirring, for 30 seconds.

Pour in half of the coconut milk and 7 tbsp water, then add the potato wedges and bring to a boil. Add the chicken pieces and simmer over a low heat for 15–20 minutes or until they are almost cooked. Add the remaining coconut milk and simmer gently until the chicken is cooked and the potatoes are tender.

In the meantime, prepare the seasoning. Heat 1 tbsp coconut oil in a separate pan and sauté the mustards seeds until they crackle. Add the sliced shallots and curry leaves, and fry gently until the shallots are softened and golden in color.

Serve the chicken curry topped with the aromatic seasoning and accompanied by rice.

2¾ lb whole chicken

SPICE POWDER:

1 star anise

3 dried red Kashmiri chili peppers*

1 tbsp coriander seeds

½ tsp ground turmeric

10 black peppercorns

6 cloves

4 green cardamom pods*

2-in piece cassia bark or cinnamon stick

TO COOK:

3 tbsp coconut oil or vegetable oil

1⅔ cups finely sliced onions

1 tbsp chopped ginger

2 tbsp chopped garlic

4 green chili peppers, slit lengthwise

1 tsp salt

1⅔ cups coconut milk*

2 small potatoes, scrubbed and cut into wedges

SEASONING:

1 tbsp coconut oil

1 tsp black mustard seeds

⅓ cup sliced shallots

25 curry leaves*

MURG MAKHAN MASALA

Chicken in spicy tomato and onion sauce

"Chicken tikka masala" was probably inspired by this north Indian classic. I cook tandoori chicken for this dish to enhance the flavors, but you may use ordinary chicken or buy ready-made tandoori chicken from your local Indian restaurant. If using raw chicken, sauté it lightly in 1 tbsp oil to seal, then cook through in the sauce.

Cut the roast chicken pieces in half, to give 8 pieces. Heat the oil in a heavy pan. Add the ginger and sauté for a minute, then add the tomatoes and 7 tbsp water. Cook over a low heat for 35–40 minutes until the tomatoes break down to form a sauce. Whiz in a blender or food processor until smooth, then strain through a fine strainer and set aside.

Heat the butter in a clean pan and sauté the onion for 3 minutes until light brown in color. Add the green chili pepper and tomato sauce. Bring to a simmer and add the fenugreek, garam masala, chili powder, honey, and salt. Simmer for 30 minutes to allow the spices to blend with the sauce, then add the cream and cook for a further 3–5 minutes.

Add the chicken pieces and simmer for 10–15 minutes until the chicken is heated through. Sprinkle with chopped cilantro and serve with pulao rice.

2¾ lb tandoori spice roasted chicken (page 71)
2 tbsp vegetable oil
2 tbsp roughly chopped peeled ginger
2¼ lb tomatoes, roughly chopped
2 tbsp butter
1 medium onion, finely sliced
1 green chili pepper, slit lengthwise
1 tsp dried fenugreek leaf powder*
1 tsp garam masala
1 tsp Kashmiri red chili powder*
2 tbsp honey
1 tsp salt, or to taste
¼ cup whipping cream
2 tbsp finely chopped cilantro leaves

MURGI JHOL

Bengali chicken stew

As an east Indian by birth, I am passionate about this recipe. The first time I made it for my cousins visiting from the Punjab, they were reluctant to eat it as they considered the sauce to be very thin and the color far too subtle – hardly a chicken curry in their view. On tasting it, they were pleasantly surprised by the flavors and delicate spicing. Now, whenever I visit them I have to cook it.

Cut the chicken into 8 pieces and remove the skin. Heat the oil in a large deep sauté pan and sauté the chicken pieces for a minute or so, without coloring. Remove from the pan and set aside.

Reheat the oil remaining in the pan. Add the panch phoran, bay leaf, cloves, and cassia or cinnamon. Sauté for 1–2 minutes, then add the ginger-garlic paste and cook, stirring, for 2–3 minutes until it loses its raw taste.

Stir in the ground spices, add the tomatoes, and sauté for 2 minutes. Add the chicken and salt, cook over a low heat for 2 minutes, then add 1⅔ cups water. Bring to a simmer and add the potatoes and cauliflower. Cook for about 20 minutes until the chicken and potatoes are cooked.

Serve sprinkled with Bengali garam masala and chopped cilantro.

2¾ lb whole chicken
⅓ cup vegetable oil
1 tsp panch phoran*
1 bay leaf
2 cloves
2-in piece cassia bark or cinnamon stick
1 tsp ginger-garlic paste*
1½ tsp ground turmeric
1 tsp ground coriander
½ tsp ground cumin
2 large tomatoes, cut into wedges
1 tsp salt, or to taste
5oz potatoes, peeled and cut into wedges
5oz cauliflower, cut into florets
¼ tsp Bengali garam masala*
1 tbsp chopped cilantro leaves

MASALEDAR BATYEREN

Spicy quails PUNJAB, NORTH INDIA

This recipe is a great favorite in the Punjab, my home state. Punjabi men love hunting, especially quail, and they usually take care of the preparation themselves. Obviously, they like to brag about their hunting and cooking skills ... whatever they might tell you, this dish is actually very simple to prepare.

Put the quails in a bowl, sprinkle with 1/2 tsp of the salt, and coat with the yogurt. Leave to marinate for about 30 minutes.

Heat the oil in a deep sauté pan. Add the coriander seeds, cardamom pods, cloves, and cassia or cinnamon, and sauté over a medium heat until they begin to crackle. Add the onions and sauté until softened and golden brown. Stir in the ginger-garlic paste and sauté for 2–3 minutes.

Add the quails and brown gently on a low heat for 3–4 minutes (without burning the onions). Add the tomatoes, remaining salt, chili powder, and coriander. Increase the heat and cook, stirring occasionally, for 15–20 minutes or until the fat starts to separate and the quails are cooked.

Adjust the seasoning. Sprinkle with garam masala and serve garnished with cilantro. Accompany with Indian bread, such as chapattis or naan.

4 quails, skinned
1 tsp salt, or to taste
1/4 cup plain yogurt
4 tbsp sunflower oil
1 tbsp coriander seeds
10 green cardamom pods*
5 cloves
2 x 1-in pieces cassia bark or cinnamon sticks
2 cups thinly sliced onions
2 tbsp ginger-garlic paste*
6 tomatoes, diced
2 tsp Kashmiri red chili powder*
2 tsp ground coriander
1 tsp garam masala
handful of cilantro sprigs, to garnish

SURTI SANTARA NA CHHAL MA BATHAK

Duck curry with orange GUJARAT, WEST INDIA

Gujarat may be a dry state, but it has a cuisine that is varied and full of flavors. In this unusual Parsi-influenced recipe, the calming orange flavor works well with the exotic warm spice blends.

Cut each duck breast into 4 or 5 pieces. Heat the oil in a large deep sauté pan, add the whole spices, and sauté until they begin to crackle. Add the sliced onions and sauté until softened and light brown in color.

Add the ginger-garlic paste and chilies; cook, stirring, for 2–3 minutes. Add the chili powder, turmeric, and cumin, and sauté for 30 seconds.

Add the duck pieces to the pan and sauté until light brown in color all over. Stir in the tomatoes and salt, then add 7 tbsp water and half of the orange juice. Bring to a simmer and cook gently for 20 minutes or until the duck is almost cooked.

In the meantime, cut the orange zest into julienne strips and blanch in boiling water for 1 minute, then drain and set aside.

Add the orange zest julienne and remaining orange juice to the pan and simmer until the duck is cooked. Correct the seasoning and sprinkle with chopped cilantro and garam masala to serve.

1 1/2 lb skinless, boneless duck breasts
7 tbsp vegetable oil
1/2 tsp cumin seeds
2-in piece cassia bark or cinnamon stick
2 cloves
4 green cardamom pods*
1 2/3 cups sliced onions
2 tsp ginger-garlic paste*
3 green chili peppers, chopped
1 tsp Kashmiri red chili powder*
1 tsp ground turmeric
2 tsp ground cumin
1/2 cup chopped fresh tomatoes
1/2 tsp salt, or to taste
1 1/4 cups orange juice
finely pared zest of 1 orange
1 tbsp cilantro leaves, chopped
1/2 tsp garam masala

PURA KICHILI PAZHAM MELAGU KARI

Pigeon cooked with Chettinad spices — TAMIL NADU, SOUTH INDIA

Pigeon is not a common game bird in Indian cuisine, but there are some interesting, unusual recipes to be found within lesser-known communities. Chettiars, for example, have always been big on game. Wild boar, pigeon, hare, and deer are among their favorites. For this recipe, you need to use wild pigeon with its highly flavored, dense flesh, rather than the milder farmed alternative; the younger the pigeon, the better the flavor and texture. Do include the liver – it enhances the flavor of the dish.

Cut each pigeon into 4 pieces (2 leg quarters and 2 breasts with wing bones attached) and remove the skin. Put the pigeon pieces in a shallow dish. Mix together the orange juice, ginger-garlic paste, turmeric, and salt, then spoon over the pigeon pieces, and turn to coat all over. Set aside to marinate in a cool place for at least 30 minutes. (Reserve the orange zest for the garnish.)

In the meantime, prepare the toasted spice powder. Dry-fry the spices in a heavy-based frying pan over a medium heat for 2–3 minutes until they crackle, shaking the pan constantly. Allow to cool, then grind to a powder, using a spice grinder, mortar and pestle, or mini-processor. Set aside.

When ready to cook, heat the oil in a pan, add the curry leaves, and sauté for a minute or two, then add the sliced onions and fry until softened and golden brown in color.

Add the toasted spice powder, sauté for a minute, then add the pigeon (including the liver) together with the marinade. Sauté for a few minutes until the pigeon pieces are lightly browned. Add 1 cup water and bring to a simmer. Cook slowly for about 45 minutes until the pigeon is tender.

Add the chopped cilantro leaves and grated orange zest. Stir well and serve hot, with chapattis.

2 wood pigeons or Cornish game hens, cleaned
   (liver reserved)
grated zest and juice of 1 orange
2 tsp ginger-garlic paste*
1/2 tsp ground turmeric
1 tsp salt

TOASTED SPICE POWDER:
1 tsp black peppercorns
1 tsp cumin seeds
2 tsp fennel seeds
1 star anise
5 green cardamom pods*
2 cloves
1-in piece cassia bark or cinnamon stick

TO COOK:
4 tbsp vegetable oil
10 curry leaves*
2 medium onions, thinly sliced
4 tbsp chopped cilantro leaves

LAGAN KA TITAR

Slow-cooked partridge NORTH INDIA

Until recently in India, *chidimaar* – or bird hunters – were very common. Most game birds were bought from these hunters, who would sell their merchandise from door to door. Since the Indian government has imposed certain restrictions on killing game, the profession has declined. This recipe is named after the dish it is traditionally cooked in – a *lagan* is a casserole with a tight-fitting lid, for slow cooking on charcoal. A well-sealed casserole in a domestic oven is just as effective. Marinating game birds prior to slow cooking helps to make them succulent and juicy.

Cut each partridge into 4 pieces (2 leg quarters and 2 breasts with wing bones attached) and remove the skin. Place in a shallow dish, spread with the ginger-garlic paste, and sprinkle with the salt. Set aside for 30 minutes.

Meanwhile, to make the spice powder, grind the spices together to a fine powder, using a spice grinder, mortar and pestle, or mini-processor. Set aside.

For the seeded coconut paste, toast the poppy seeds, coconut, and melon or pumpkin seeds together in a dry frying pan over a medium heat until golden. Cool slightly, then put into a blender or mini-processor with 2 tbsp water and whiz to a fine paste.

Mix the spice paste, seeded coconut paste, yogurt, and fried onion paste together in a large casserole with a tight-fitting lid. Stir in the remaining marinating ingredients with 3 cups water. Add the partridge pieces, turn to coat, cover, and set aside to marinate for 30 minutes. Meanwhile, preheat the oven to 340°F (300°F convection oven).

Mix a cupful of flour with enough water to make a paste, and spread around the rim of the casserole to seal the lid. Cook in the oven for 35–45 minutes or until the partridge is tender. Serve sprinkled with chopped cilantro leaves.

2 partridges or pheasants, cleaned

1½ tbsp ginger-garlic paste*

1 tsp salt

SPICE POWDER:

1 tsp black peppercorns

1 black cardamom pod*

6 green cardamom pods*

1-in piece cassia bark or cinnamon stick

¼ tsp freshly grated nutmeg

SEEDED COCONUT PASTE:

1 tbsp white poppy seeds

5 tbsp unsweetened dried, shredded coconut*, toasted

2 tbsp melon seeds or pumpkin seeds, toasted

TO MARINATE:

1 cup thick yogurt

6 tbsp fried onion paste*

7 tbsp butter, melted

3–5 cloves

1 bay leaf

1½ tbsp slivered almonds

1½ tbsp slivered pistachios

5–6 saffron threads, infused in 1 tbsp milk

1 tbsp kewra water (screwpine flower essence)*

GARNISH:

1 tbsp chopped cilantro leaves

MEAT

Prior to Muslim invasions, the British Raj, and other foreign influences, meat was eaten by the warrior clans only, as the rest of the Indian community was purely vegetarian. These days, more people eat meat. Lamb is popular in Kashmir, but elsewhere goat is the predominant meat, as beef and pork are rarely eaten. Venison only features on restaurant menus and lavish tables. Indians eat their meat well cooked – just cooked or underdone is not a concept in Indian cooking. As you travel from region to region, you find fascinating differences in cooking techniques, especially with spicing.

ROGAN JOSH

Kashmiri lamb curry · KASHMIR, NORTH INDIA

Rogan josh **is a classical preparation, traditionally made with lamb, and only lamb. There are various claims to the origin of the name. Some claim that the violet bark of a Kashmiri tree called** *ratanjog* **should be boiled in oil to prepare** *rogan***, and this oil is used to make the curry. Others say** *rogan* **simply describes red colored chili oil that floats on the surface of the dish. Recently, I met up with some old school friends from Kashmiri who informed me that** *marwal ka phool* **(cock's comb flower extract) should be used to give** *rogan josh* **its characteristic color. To keep it simple, I use the color from red chili peppers and tomato paste to give the right appearance. The inclusion of almonds is another source of controversy. I marinate the lamb in a mixture of crushed almonds, saffron, and yogurt to create a canvas for the spectrum of spice flavors that follows during the cooking. It also makes sense to use local ingredients indigenous to Kashmir for a classic recipe of the state.**

Put the lamb into a shallow dish. For the marinade, whisk the yogurt with the saffron and almonds. Add to the lamb, turn to coat, and set aside to marinate in a cool place for 2 hours.

To prepare the garam masala, pound the spices together to a powder, using a spice grinder, mortar and pestle, or mini-processor.

Heat the oil in a heavy-based pan, add the pounded garam masala, and stir until the spices start to crackle. Add the sliced onions, stir, and cook for 8–12 minutes until softened and golden brown. Add the ginger-garlic paste and sauté for 2–3 minutes.

Add the lamb, together with the marinade, stir, and cook for about 30 minutes until the meat is browned and three-quarters cooked. (The lamb will cook in its own juices, but if there is very little liquid in the pan, some water or lamb stock can be added. Once the meat is browned, it will tend to stick to the bottom of the pan, so keep stirring and scraping the bottom – this is important to develop the characteristic flavor.)

Add the chili powder and ground spices, and cook for 3–5 minutes, adding a little water if required. Stir in the salt and tomato paste, and cook, stirring, until the lamb is tender. Finally, stir in the chopped cilantro.

Serve garnished with red chilies, and accompanied by cilantro chutney and saffron rice or an Indian bread.

2¼ lb leg of lamb, cut into 2-in pieces, on the bone

MARINADE:
⅔ cup plain whole milk yogurt, lightly whisked
pinch of saffron threads
2 tbsp finely crushed blanched almonds

GARAM MASALA:
1½ tsp cumin seeds
6 green cardamom pods*
2 black cardamom pods*
1-in piece cassia bark or cinnamon stick
8 cloves
2 mace
1 tbsp black peppercorns

TO COOK:
6 tbsp vegetable oil
3 cups finely sliced onions
2 tbsp ginger-garlic paste*
1½ tsp Kashmiri red chili powder*
2 tbsp ground coriander
1 tsp garam masala
1 tsp ground turmeric
½ tsp salt, or to taste
2 tbsp tomato paste
3 tbsp finely chopped cilantro leaves

TO SERVE:
dried red Kashmiri chili peppers*
cilantro chutney (page 138)

VADAMA KARI KOZHAMBU

Almond lamb curry TAMIL NADU, SOUTH INDIA

Traditionally, this preparation takes its flavor from *vadagam* – a powdered, sun-dried blend of lentils and spices, which is tedious to make at home. Some Asian grocers stock it, but for this recipe I have simplified the flavors and used whole spices – it works well.

Cut the lamb into 1½-in pieces. Soak the almonds in warm water to cover for 10 minutes, then drain and blend to a paste with the poppy seeds, using a blender or mini-processor. Soak the tamarind pulp in 4 tbsp warm water for 20 minutes, then strain through a fine strainer.

Heat the oil in a deep sauté pan, add the whole spices and curry leaves, and sauté until the spices crackle. Add the chopped onions and fry until softened and golden brown in color. Add the ginger-garlic paste and cook, stirring, for 2–3 minutes to lose the raw taste.

Add the tomatoes and cook for about 10 minutes. Stir in the ground spices and cook, stirring, for 2–3 minutes, adding a little water if needed.

Add the lamb and sauté to seal on all sides. Add salt and 1 cup water. Cook over a low heat for 30 minutes. Stir in the almond paste and tamarind liquid, and simmer for 15 minutes or until the lamb is cooked, adding a little water if the sauce is too thick. Serve scattered with almonds and cilantro.

1lb 2oz boneless leg of lamb
1¼ cups blanched almonds
2 tsp poppy seeds
2 tbsp tamarind pulp*
2 tbsp oil
3 cloves
2 cinnamon sticks
3 green cardamom pods*
8 curry leaves*
2 medium onions, chopped
2 tsp ginger-garlic paste*
2 medium tomatoes, chopped
½ tsp ground turmeric
3 tsp ground coriander
2 tsp Kashmiri red chili powder*
1 tsp salt, or to taste
20 almond slivers, lightly toasted
cilantro sprigs, to garnish

GHAZAALA

Lamb with green chilies HYDERABAD, SOUTH INDIA

Most of the heat in chili peppers comes from the seeds and white membrane. Remove these to reduce the heat by about 80%, yet still provide a great flavor kick. Fat chilies are less fiery but flavorful – essential for recipes calling for green chili flavor rather than heat.

Cut the lamb into 1-in cubes. Whiz half the chili peppers in a blender to a paste, then pour into a bowl, and mix with the yogurt, turmeric, crushed coriander, and salt. Cover and set aside.

Heat the oil in a deep sauté pan and sauté the remaining chili peppers for 2 minutes; remove and keep aside. Sauté the sliced onions in the oil remaining in the pan until softened and light brown in color.

Add the lamb and sauté until browned on all sides. Cook gently, stirring frequently, for 15–20 minutes to evaporate all the juices. Add the ginger-garlic paste and sauté well for 2–3 minutes to lose the raw taste.

Add the yogurt mixture with 1 cup water and simmer for 20 minutes or until the lamb is cooked. Add the fried chili peppers and chopped cilantro and simmer for a few minutes. Add the lime zest and juice. Serve with rice.

1lb 2oz boneless leg of lamb
5 fat green chili peppers, slit lengthwise and seeded
⅞ cup plain whole milk yogurt
1 tsp ground turmeric
3 tsp coriander seeds, toasted and roughly crushed
1 tsp salt, or to taste
4 tbsp vegetable oil
1½ lb onions, thinly sliced
2 tsp ginger-garlic paste*
4 tbsp chopped cilantro leaves
grated zest and juice of 3 limes

SALLI MA KHARU GOSHT

Parsi lamb curry with straw potatoes WEST INDIA

This has been a favorite Parsi dish in Indian restaurants for a long time. It's a great recipe, without a great deal of ingredients, and cooks well. The presentation is dramatic, but adds to the appeal.

Cut the lamb into 1½-in cubes. Heat the oil in a deep sauté pan and sauté the whole spices and dried whole chili pepper until they crackle. Add the sliced onions and fry until softened and golden brown in color.

Add 3 tbsp water and simmer until the water evaporates, then add the ginger-garlic paste and sauté for 2 minutes to lose the raw taste. Add the turmeric, cumin, chili powder, and salt, and cook, stirring, for 1 minute.

Add the lamb, together with the chopped tomatoes if using, and sauté for 3–5 minutes until well browned. Add the green chili peppers and 7 tbsp water, and bring to a simmer. Cook over a low heat, stirring frequently, for 40 minutes until the lamb is cooked.

Meanwhile, for the garnish, peel the potatoes and cut into fine strips; pat dry on paper towel. Heat the oil for deep-frying in a suitable pan to 375°F, and deep-fry the potatoes in small batches for 2–3 minutes until crisp and golden. Remove with a slotted spoon and drain on paper towel.

Spoon the curry into bowls and sprinkle with the shredded cilantro. Pile the fried julienne potatoes on top and serve.

1lb 2oz boneless leg of lamb
4 tbsp vegetable oil
1-in piece cassia bark or cinnamon stick
2 cloves
3 green cardamom pods*
1 small dried red Kashmiri chili pepper*
3 large onions, sliced
1½ tsp ginger-garlic paste*
1 tsp ground turmeric
2 tsp ground cumin
1 tsp Kashmiri red chili powder*
1 tsp salt
2 tomatoes, chopped (optional)
3 green chili peppers, slit lengthwise and seeded

GARNISH:
2 potatoes, cut into julienne
vegetable oil, to deep-fry
shredded cilantro leaves

KOSHA MANGSHO

Dry lamb curry WEST BENGAL, EAST INDIA

This easy curry will satisfy a craving for spicy thick gravy with lots of meat essence. *Sukha gosht* and *bhuna gosht* are similar dry, spicy preparations but this recipe has its regional characteristics. It is perfect with thin chapattis, or you could serve it with tortilla bread.

Put the lamb into a shallow dish. Mix the yogurt with the salt and turmeric, add to the lamb, and turn to coat all over. Set aside to marinate in a cool place for 45 minutes.

Heat the oil in a deep sauté pan, add the onions, and sauté until softened and lightly colored. Add the lamb with the marinade and sauté to seal and brown on all sides.

Add the ginger-garlic paste and sauté for 2–3 minutes to lose the raw taste, then add the ground spices and sauté for a minute. Stir in the tomato paste and 1¼ cups water. Bring to a simmer and cook over a low heat for about 40 minutes until the lamb is cooked.

Serve hot, sprinkled with garam masala and chopped cilantro.

2¼ lb leg of lamb, cut into 2-in pieces, on the bone
½ cup plain yogurt
1 tsp salt, or to taste
1 tsp ground turmeric
6 tbsp vegetable oil
1¼ cups sliced onions
3 tsp ginger-garlic paste*
2½ tsp ground coriander
2 tsp ground cumin
1½ tsp Kashmiri red chili powder*
1 tbsp tomato paste, or 2 chopped tomatoes
½ tsp Bengali garam masala*
1 tbsp cilantro leaves, chopped

CHAAP KARI VARUVAL

Lamb chop curry TAMIL NADU, SOUTH INDIA

This recipe belongs to a region where I would like be born again. The cuisine is so intricate that it is said you must be born Chettiar to be able to cook the food properly. Nattulkotai Chettiars were a nomadic trading community that once roamed and sailed through south India and southeast Asian countries assimilating local foods, such as sticky red rice, into their own cuisine. Their unusual spices are *kalpasi*, a stone fungus, and *marathi mukka*, buds from a local tree akin to cloves. These give characteristic flavor to Chettinad dishes, but they are not available here, so I have developed a similar flavor profile using simple spices.

Trim as much fat as possible from the lamb chops. Cut and scrape all the fat off the rib bones from the meat to the tips. Flatten the lamb chops with a wooden mallet and place in a shallow dish. Combine the yogurt, turmeric, and salt. Coat the lamb chops with the spiced yogurt and set aside in a cool place to marinate for 1 hour.

To make the spice paste, heat the 1 tbsp oil in a frying pan, add the whole spices, and sauté until they crackle. Add the sliced onion and sauté until softened and golden brown. Add the ginger-garlic paste and cook for a few minutes to lose the raw aroma. Add the tomatoes and green chili peppers, and cook until the fat separates from the mixture. Stir in the chopped cilantro and set aside for 5 minutes to cool slightly. Transfer to a blender and process to a fine paste. Pour into a bowl and set aside.

For the seasoning, heat the 2½ tbsp oil in a deep sauté pan and sauté the bay leaves, cassia or cinnamon, cardamom pod, and clove for 1 minute. Add the sliced onions and cook until translucent. Add the spice paste and sauté until golden in color.

Add the lamb chops and continue cooking until the oil starts to separate from the spice paste. Add the lime juice, check the seasoning, and continue to cook until the chops are tender.

Arrange the chops in a warmed serving dish and garnish with chopped cilantro and ginger julienne to serve.

1lb lamb rib chops

2 tbsp plain whole milk yogurt

1 tsp ground turmeric

1 tsp salt, or to taste

1 tbsp lime juice

SPICE PASTE:

1 tbsp oil

2 tsp coriander seeds

1 tsp black peppercorns

1 tsp fennel seeds

3 cloves

1-in piece cassia bark or cinnamon stick

2 green cardamom pods

1 medium onion, finely sliced

1 tbsp ginger-garlic paste*

2 tomatoes, roughly chopped

4 green chili peppers, finely chopped

4 tbsp cilantro leaves, finely chopped

SEASONING:

2½ tbsp oil

2 bay leaves

1-in piece cassia bark or cinnamon stick

1 green cardamom pod*

1 clove

2 medium onions, sliced

GARNISH:

chopped cilantro

ginger julienne

RAAN E SIKANDER

Spiced roast leg of lamb NORTH INDIA

This is a traditional recipe with Afghan influence. The combination of braising and roasting makes the lamb really succulent and juicy.

Make a few deep cuts in the surface of the lamb. Mix the ginger-garlic paste with 1½ tsp chili powder and 3 tbsp oil, and massage over the lamb and into the cuts. Marinate at room temperature for 2 hours, then in the fridge for another 2 hours. Preheat oven to 340°F (300°F convection oven).

Heat the remaining oil in a flameproof casserole large enough to hold the lamb. Add the whole spices and bay leaf. Sauté for 1 minute, then add the onions and cook until softened. Stir in the remaining 1 tsp chili powder and other ground spices and sauté until the oil separates.

Stir in the tomato paste and salt, then add the leg of lamb. Seal the pan with foil and a lid, and cook in the oven for 50 minutes to 1½ hours until the lamb is very tender, turning it once or twice during cooking.

Preheat broiler. Remove lamb from casserole and broil for a few minutes, turning to lightly char the surface. Meanwhile, bubble the sauce on the stove to reduce, then strain. Carve the lamb and serve with the sauce.

1 small leg of lamb, about 2¼ lb, trimmed
4 tbsp ginger-garlic paste*
2½ tsp Kashmiri red chili powder*
8 tbsp vegetable oil
3 cloves
4 green cardamom pods*
3 black cardamom pods*
2-in piece cassia bark or cinnamon stick
2 star anise
1 bay leaf
4 medium onions, finely sliced
2 tsp ground coriander
2 tsp ground cumin
1 tsp ground turmeric
1 tbsp tomato paste
1 tsp salt, or to taste

KAIRI KA GOSHT DO PIAZA

Lamb in mango and onion sauce SOUTH INDIA

Do-piaza **implies the addition of onions to a dish twice. Lucknow and Hyderabad both claim the authentic version; I have chosen the Hyderabadi version because of the interesting inclusion of mango.**

Cut the lamb into 1-in cubes. Whiz half of the onions in a blender or food processor to make a smooth paste. Slice the remaining onions.

Heat the oil in a deep sauté pan and fry the sliced onions until softened and golden brown; remove and set aside. Add the onion paste and sauté for 3–5 minutes until golden brown. Stir in the ginger-garlic paste and cook well for 2–3 minutes. Add the ground spices and sauté for 30 seconds.

Add the lamb and salt, and cook, stirring, for 3–5 minutes until lightly browned. Add 7 tbsp water and simmer for a few minutes, then add the mango, sugar, and chili peppers. Cook gently for 30 minutes or until the lamb is almost tender, adding a little more water if needed.

Meanwhile, whiz the cilantro leaves to a paste in a blender. Stir into the sauce with the curry leaves and simmer for a further 10 minutes.

For the seasoning, heat the 1 tbsp oil in another pan and fry the mustard seeds, chilies, and garlic until lightly browned. Pour over the lamb, cover, and serve immediately to retain the flavors. Serve with Indian bread.

1½ lb boneless leg of lamb
4 medium onions
5 tbsp vegetable oil
1 tbsp ginger-garlic paste*
½ tsp ground turmeric
1 tsp garam masala
1 tsp Kashmiri red chili powder*
1 tsp salt
1 mango, peeled and cut into julienne
1 tsp sugar
3 green chili peppers, finely chopped
1 cup cilantro leaves
10 curry leaves*, roughly chopped

SEASONING:
1 tbsp oil
1 tsp black mustard seeds
2 green chili peppers, slit lengthwise
4 garlic cloves, sliced

MARATHI NALLI GOSHT

Marathi-style lamb shank SHOLAPUR, WEST INDIA

The textures and flavors are wonderfully varied in this region, and the spicing is quite unique. Peanuts, sesame seeds, red chilies, onions, and garlic are some of the common flavorings. This recipe belongs to the Maratha warriors, as they were the privileged clan who were allowed to eat meat.

Put the lamb shanks into a shallow dish. Mix together the ingredients for the marinade and apply to the lamb shanks, massaging well. Cover and leave to marinate in the fridge for 4–6 hours.

To prepare the roasted spice blend, dry-fry the dried chili peppers, spices, and sesame seeds in a heavy-based frying pan over a medium heat for 2–3 minutes until they crackle, shaking the pan constantly. Allow to cool, then grind to a powder, using a spice grinder, mortar and pestle, or mini-processor; set aside.

For the sauce, thinly slice two of the onions; finely chop the other one and set aside. Heat the oil in a flameproof casserole or heavy-based deep pan. Add the sliced onions and fry until softened and golden. Add the chopped onion and sauté until softened and brown in color, then add the ginger-garlic paste and sauté for 2–3 minutes to lose the raw taste. Stir in the turmeric and roasted spice blend and sauté for 30 seconds.

Add the lamb shanks to the pan and sauté to seal all over, then add the tomato paste, salt, and 7 tbsp water and bring to a simmer, stirring. Cover and cook over a low heat or transfer to a preheated oven at 360°F (325°F convection oven) and cook for about 45 minutes until the lamb shanks are tender. Uncover for the final 10 minutes' cooking.

Remove the lamb shanks from the sauce and place on a warmed platter; keep warm. Whiz the sauce in a blender until smooth, then pass through a strainer into a clean pan and reheat gently. Finally, stir in the chopped cilantro.

Serve the lamb shanks with the sauce poured over, and garnished with shredded green onion.

2 lamb shanks

MARINADE:

1 tsp dried chili flakes

1 tbsp ginger-garlic paste*

1/2 tsp ground turmeric

3 tbsp plain yogurt

1 tbsp lime juice

2 tbsp vegetable oil

ROASTED SPICE BLEND:

4 small dried red Kashmiri chili peppers*

2-in piece cassia bark or cinnamon stick

8 cloves

8 green cardamom pods*

2 black cardamom pods*

2 tbsp coriander seeds

1 tsp sesame seeds

SAUCE:

3 large onions

5 tbsp vegetable oil

1 1/2 tbsp ginger-garlic paste*

1 1/2 tsp ground turmeric

1 tbsp tomato paste

1/2 tsp salt, or to taste

1 tbsp chopped cilantro leaves

GARNISH:

shredded green onion

MANGSHO GHUGNI

Lamb curry with chickpeas BENGAL, EAST INDIA

***Mangsho* is meat and generally meat for the people of Hindu Bengali origin is *panther*, which is goat meat. This traditional curry is normally made with diced meat, though here I have used lamb steaks. I like to cook the chickpeas, but you can use canned ones.**

Drain the chickpeas, put into a saucepan, and cover with fresh water. Add 1 bay leaf, 1 clove, and 1 cardamom pod, and bring to a boil. Lower the heat and simmer until the chickpeas are cooked, about 2 hours. Season with ½ tsp of the salt toward the end of cooking. Drain and set aside.

Heat the oil in a deep sauté pan. Add the remaining bay leaves, cloves, and cardamom pods and sauté until they crackle. Add the onions and sauté until softened and translucent. Add the ginger-garlic paste and cook, stirring, for 2–3 minutes. Add the ground coriander, chili powder, and cumin and stir for 30 seconds.

Add the tomatoes, lamb steaks, salt, and just enough water to cover the mixture. Cook gently for about 30 minutes. Add the chickpeas and simmer for a further 5 minutes or until the lamb is cooked. Serve sprinkled with garam masala. Garnish with chopped cilantro and ginger julienne.

1 cup chickpeas, soaked in cold water overnight

3 bay leaves

7 cloves

4 black cardamom pods*

1 tsp salt, or to taste

6 tbsp vegetable oil or mustard oil

1⅔ cups finely sliced onions

1½ tbsp ginger-garlic paste*

1 tsp ground coriander

1 tsp Kashmiri red chili powder*

1 tsp ground cumin

1 cup finely chopped fresh tomatoes

4 lamb leg steaks, each about 3½ oz

GARNISH:

½ tsp Bengali garam masala*

chopped cilantro leaves

ginger julienne

ALOO GOSHT SALAN

Lamb with potatoes BIHAR, EAST INDIA

Cooking lamb with potatoes is very common in eastern India. This tempting recipe is almost like a spicy stew – the potatoes absorb the lamb juices to delicious effect.

Cut the lamb into 1½-in cubes. Heat the oil in a deep heavy-based sauté pan and add the chopped ginger. Sauté for 30 seconds, then add the bay leaves, cloves, cardamom pods, and cumin seeds, and sauté well until the spices crackle. Add the onions and fry until softened and golden brown.

Add the lamb and sauté well for 10–12 minutes to seal and brown on all sides. Stir in the chili powder, coriander, and turmeric. Add the potato wedges and sauté for 2–3 minutes. Add 1 cup water and the salt. Bring to a simmer and cook gently for about 15 minutes until the potatoes are nearly tender.

Meanwhile, cut the green onions into 1-in lengths and the red bell pepper into wide strips. Add to the pan with the tomatoes and cook for a further 5–10 minutes until the lamb is tender.

Serve sprinkled with garam masala and chopped cilantro. Accompany with boiled rice or an Indian bread.

1½ lb boneless leg of lamb

4 tbsp vegetable oil

2 tbsp finely chopped ginger

2 bay leaves

4 cloves

2 black cardamom pods*

1½ tsp cumin seeds

4 medium onions, finely sliced

1 tsp Kashmiri red chili powder*

1½ tsp ground coriander

1½ tsp ground turmeric

2 medium potatoes, scrubbed and cut into wedges

½ tsp salt, or to taste

4 green onions, trimmed

1 red bell pepper, cored and seeded

3 medium tomatoes, cut into wedges

½ tsp garam masala

1 tbsp chopped cilantro leaves

ERACHI OLARTHIYATHU

Syrian Christian lamb curry KERALA, SOUTH INDIA

At my chef school I was really impressed with Chef George K. George who was one year my senior. I caught up with George in Kochi in 2002. He had not changed a bit since college days – same cool, easy attitude, a very contented soul. George has been a great influence on my learning of Keralan food. He is a dedicated Syrian Christian and a true chef. I have tried to recreate his beef curry as a lamb curry – it's a great recipe ... by George!

Cut the lamb into 1-in cubes. Put the ingredients for the spice paste in a blender or mini-processor and grind to a fine paste.

Put the lamb into a heavy-based pan with the spice paste, sliced onion and garlic, ginger julienne, curry leaves, coconut slices, salt, and 3–4 tbsp water. Bring to a simmer and cook gently for 35–40 minutes, stirring frequently, until the meat is tender.

For the final spicing, heat the oil in a separate pan and sauté the onions with the curry leaves until the onions are softened and brown in color. Add this spicing to the meat and cook slowly for a further 5–7 minutes. Serve garnished with chopped cilantro leaves.

1lb 2oz boneless leg of lamb

SPICE PASTE:
1 tsp Kashmiri red chili powder*
2 tsp ground coriander
$1/2$ tsp ground turmeric
$1/2$ tsp cumin seeds
$1/2$ tsp black peppercorns
2 star anise
1-in piece cassia bark or cinnamon stick
2 cloves
2 green cardamom pods*
3 tbsp white vinegar

TO COOK:
1 medium onion, sliced
2 garlic cloves, sliced
1-in piece ginger, peeled and cut into julienne
10 curry leaves*
$2/3$ cup thinly sliced fresh coconut*
1 tsp salt, or to taste

FINAL SPICING:
4 tbsp vegetable oil
2 medium onions, thinly sliced
10 curry leaves*

GARNISH:
2 tbsp chopped cilantro leaves

MAMSA ISHTEW

Aromatic stew with coconut milk   KARNATAKA, SOUTH INDIA

This beautiful lamb stew is a speciality of Mangalore and the Karvari coast – a very colorful part of Karnataka with a wide spectrum of flavors. The community in Mangalore is predominantly Catholic and prepares some of the hottest and the mildest food of India. The list of ingredients can be a little intimidating, but the result is spectacular and you'll probably find you have most of the spices already. Almost every south Indian state will have its own version of lamb stew – this is one of my favorites.

Cut the lamb into 1½-in cubes and place in a deep heavy-based pan with the coconut milk, three-quarters of the ginger julienne, the lemon juice, and salt. Simmer for about 30 minutes until the lamb is three-quarters cooked.

Meanwhile, heat the oil in a separate pan and sauté the garlic gently for a minute without coloring. Add the curry leaves, whole spices, and bay leaves, and sauté until the spices crackle.

Add the sliced onions and green chili peppers and fry gently until the onion is softened, but not colored. Add the peppercorns, turmeric, cumin, and fennel, and sauté for 30 seconds or so. Add the potatoes and sauté for 8–10 minutes until sealed and golden brown on all sides.

Add the spice mixture to the lamb and stir well. Cook on a low heat for a further 15–20 minutes until the lamb is very tender. Garnish with the remaining ginger julienne to serve.

1lb 2oz boneless leg of lamb

1²/₃ cups coconut milk*

1-in piece ginger, peeled and cut into julienne

2 tsp lemon juice

1 tsp salt, or to taste

3 tbsp vegetable oil

6 garlic cloves, sliced

10 curry leaves*

1 star anise

2-in piece cassia bark or cinnamon stick

8 cloves

5 green cardamom pods*

2 bay leaves

2 medium onions, thinly sliced

2 green chili peppers, slit lengthwise

½ tsp black peppercorns

1 tsp ground turmeric

2 tsp ground cumin

2 tsp ground fennel

4 small waxy potatoes, scrubbed and halved

LAAL MAAS

Rajasthani red lamb curry RAJASTHAN, NORTH INDIA

This curry is prepared with red chili paste and the authentic dish is very hot – even hotter than "British vindaloo". I have adjusted the recipe to suit most palates. In India, goat meat would normally feature, but I have used lamb in my recipes. For this curry, you could use any meat.

Trim the lamb, if necessary. Whisk together the yogurt, crushed dried chili peppers and cumin seeds, ground spices, and salt in a bowl; set aside.

Heat the oil in a deep sauté pan and sauté the garlic until light brown in color. Add all the cardamom pods and sauté until they crackle. Add the sliced onions and fry, stirring, until softened and light brown in color.

Add the lamb and sauté over a medium heat to seal and lightly color. Add the tomato paste and stir over a low heat for 10 minutes.

Add the spiced yogurt, stir and cook on a low heat for 30–40 minutes or until the lamb is tender. Adjust the seasoning. Stir in the chopped cilantro.

Serve topped with a spoonful of spiced raita.

Spiced raita: Mix 1/4 cup thick yogurt with 1 tsp chopped cilantro, 1/4 tsp toasted cumin seeds, and a pinch of crushed dried chili flakes.

2 1/4 lb leg of lamb, cut into 2-in pieces, on the bone
1 cup plain yogurt
10 small dried red Kashmiri chili peppers*, crushed
1 tsp cumin seeds, toasted and lightly crushed
3 tsp ground coriander
1 tsp ground turmeric
1 tsp garam masala
1 tsp salt
5 tbsp vegetable oil
12 garlic cloves, sliced
5 black cardamom pods*
5 green cardamom pods*
3 medium onions, finely sliced
2 tbsp tomato paste
2 tbsp chopped cilantro leaves
spiced raita (see left), to serve

KHEEMA MATTAR

Ground lamb with peas and cumin NORTH INDIA

Indians are very fond of cooking ground meat with vegetables. I particularly like lamb cooked with green peas or potatoes, as I serve in my restaurant. You could vary the vegetable, cut into small pieces.

Finely grind the lamb, using a meat grinder, food processor, or knife, and set aside. Heat the oil in a deep sauté pan and sauté the whole spices, bay leaf, and crushed black pepper until they crackle. Add the chopped onions and sauté until softened and light brown in color.

Add the ginger-garlic paste and cook well for 2–3 minutes, then add the green chili peppers, ground lamb, and salt. Cook, stirring, for 3–5 minutes until the meat is evenly colored.

Add the tomato paste and 1 cup water, and bring to a simmer. Cook gently for 15–20 minutes until the lamb is cooked. Add the peas and cook for a further 5–10 minutes until they are tender.

Serve sprinkled with the garam masala and chopped cilantro leaves. Accompany with chapattis or any other Indian bread.

1 lb 2oz boneless leg of lamb
6 tbsp vegetable oil
3 cloves
2 green cardamom pods*
1-in piece cassia bark or cinnamon stick
1 bay leaf
1 tsp crushed black pepper
2 medium onions, finely chopped
2 tsp ginger-garlic paste*
5 green chili peppers, slit lengthwise
1 tsp salt
3 tbsp tomato paste
1 cup shelled green peas
1/2 tsp garam masala
2 tbsp chopped cilantro leaves

GOSHT KI BIRYANI

Lamb cooked with rice NORTH INDIA

There are communities in India that specialize in cooking biryani and practice it professionally. In Matka Peer in New Delhi, for example, people leave their cooking pots with chefs in the morning and collect their biryani in the evening – after it has cooked slowly on charcoal ashes for 3–4 hours. Lucknow and Hyderabad are particularly renowned for biryani cooking.

Of the various methods of cooking this dish, I have given a simple one that ensures the rice and lamb are both cooked properly. It can be served as a meal in itself, with a simple raita.

Cut the lamb into 1-in cubes and place in a shallow dish.

For the marinade, heat the oil and deep-fry the onions until crisp and brown, drain on paper towel, and cool. Put the cooled onions in a blender and whiz to a paste, then add the yogurt with the rest of the marinade ingredients and process briefly until smooth. Coat the lamb with the mixture and leave to marinate in a cool place for 2 hours.

To cook, heat 2 tbsp of the oil in a heavy-based pan and sauté the whole dried red chili peppers for 1 minute. Add the lamb with its marinade and cook on a low heat for 45 minutes, or until the meat is tender.

Meanwhile, heat the remaining 3 tbsp oil in another pan and sauté the whole spices and crushed peppercorns for a minute until they splutter. Add the rice and sauté for 2 minutes, then add 6 cups cold water. Bring to a boil and boil for 12–15 minutes until the rice is almost cooked.

Preheat the oven to 360°F (325°F convection oven). Drain the rice and spread to a 1-in thickness on a tray. Allow to cool slightly, then pick out the cassia or cinnamon, cardamom pods, and cloves.

In the meantime, for the assembly, deep-fry the onion until crisp and brown; drain on paper towel. Deep-fry the nuts, and raisins if using, until the nuts are light brown and the raisins are plump; drain.

Brush another heavy-based pan with a little melted butter and add half of the cooked lamb in a single layer. Cover with a layer of rice, 1-in thick, and sprinkle with garam masala and melted butter. Repeat these layers once more, then drizzle the saffron milk over the top layer of rice. Scatter the fried nuts and crisp-fried onion over the surface, cover tightly, and place in the oven for 20 minutes. Uncover, fork through to mix, then sprinkle with the mint and cilantro leaves. Serve at once, garnished with tomato strips and accompanied by the raita.

Cucumber and mint raita: Lightly whisk 1 cup thick whole milk yogurt, then stir in 1/4 tsp salt, 1/2 tsp toasted cumin seeds, 1 tbsp diced red onion, 1 tbsp chopped mint leaves, and 1 tbsp grated, peeled cucumber.

1lb 2oz lean boneless leg of lamb

MARINADE:
oil, to deep-fry
6 medium onions, finely sliced
1 cup plain yogurt, whisked
1 tbsp ginger-garlic paste*
1 tsp ground turmeric
1 tsp salt

TO COOK:
5 tbsp vegetable oil
3 dried red Kashmiri chili peppers*
2-in piece cassia bark or cinnamon stick
6 green cardamom pods*
1 tsp cumin seeds
4 cloves
10 black peppercorns, crushed
2³/₄ cups basmati rice, washed and drained

TO ASSEMBLE:
1 small onion, thinly sliced
2 tbsp mixed almonds, cashew nuts, and raisins
   (optional)
3 tbsp melted butter, plus more for brushing
2 tsp garam masala
pinch of saffron threads, infused in 7 tbsp warm milk
1 tbsp finely chopped mint leaves
1 tbsp chopped cilantro leaves

TO SERVE:
tomato strips, to garnish
cucumber and mint raita (see left)

BOLINAS DE CARNE EM CARIL VERDE

Goan lamb meatball green curry GOA, WEST INDIA

The key to a good meatball curry is a smooth-textured meat mixture with subtle spicing – the flavor of the meat should shine through the spices.

To make the cilantro paste, first soak the tamarind pulp in 5 tbsp warm water for 20 minutes.

For the meatballs, finely grind the lamb using a meat grinder, food processor, or knife. Put in a bowl and combine with the bread crumbs, cumin, mace, and salt until evenly blended, then shape into small balls the size of a walnut.

Strain the tamarind through a fine strainer and pour the liquid into a blender or mini-processor. Add the chopped cilantro, salt, green chili peppers, and ginger, and whiz to a paste; set aside.

To make the sauce, heat the oil in a deep sauté pan. Add the garlic and sauté briefly, then add the onions and sauté until softened and light brown in color. Add the ground coriander and cumin, and sauté for 30 seconds, then add the coconut milk and bring to a simmer.

Stir in the cilantro paste and simmer gently for 3–5 minutes. Add the meatballs and simmer slowly for about 20 minutes until they are cooked.

In the meantime, toast the ingredients for the spice powder in a heavy-based frying pan over a medium heat for 2–3 minutes until they crackle, shaking the pan constantly. Cool slightly, then grind to a powder, using a spice grinder, mini-processor, or mortar and pestle.

Sprinkle the toasted spice powder over the meatball curry and simmer for 5 minutes. Serve with boiled rice.

MEATBALLS:

1lb 2oz lean boneless leg of lamb

1 cup fresh bread crumbs

1 tsp toasted cumin seeds, ground

pinch of ground mace

1/2 tsp salt

CILANTRO PASTE:

2 tbsp tamarind pulp*

6 tbsp chopped cilantro leaves

1 tsp salt

3 green chili peppers

1 tbsp chopped ginger

SAUCE:

1 1/2 tbsp vegetable oil

1 tsp finely chopped garlic

1 cup finely chopped onions

1/2 tsp ground coriander

1/2 tsp ground cumin

1 1/4 cups coconut milk*

TOASTED SPICE POWDER:

6 peppercorns

1-in cinnamon stick

4 green cardamom pods*

HIRAN TARIWALA

Venison with winter vegetables EAST INDIA

This warming dish is based on an old family recipe that my father used to cook lamb. I find it works well with venison and has been a favorite on my winter menus for several years.

Cut the venison into 1-in cubes. Pound the whole spices together using a mortar and pestle or spice grinder until coarsely ground.

Heat the oil in a deep heavy-based pan, add the ground spices and stir until the mixture changes color and crackles. Add the chopped onions and sauté until softened and golden brown.

Add the ginger-garlic paste and cook, stirring continuously, for 2–3 minutes – keep scraping the bottom of the pan to avoid burning.

Add the venison and sauté to seal on all sides, taking care not to burn the onions. Stir in the chili powder and ground spices. Cook over a low heat for about 30 minutes until the venison is three-quarters cooked.

In the meantime, whiz the tomatoes to a purée in a blender and strain to remove seeds, if wished; set aside. Blanch the vegetables separately in boiling salted water for 3–5 minutes until *al dente*; drain.

Add the puréed tomatoes to the venison, stir, then add the blanched vegetables. Cook gently for a further 15 minutes or until the venison is tender. Sprinkle with the garam masala and chopped cilantro to serve.

1½ lb boneless leg of venison, trimmed
1 cinnamon stick
4 cloves
6 green cardamom pods*
1 tsp whole black peppercorns
1½ tsp cumin seeds
6 tbsp vegetable oil
3 medium onions, finely chopped
3 tsp ginger-garlic paste*
1 tbsp Kashmiri red chili powder*
1 tbsp ground coriander
1 tbsp ground turmeric
3½ oz tomatoes
3½ oz thin green beans, cut into 2-in lengths
12 baby turnips, scraped
12 baby carrots, scraped
20 pearl onions, peeled
salt
½ tsp garam masala, to garnish
chopped cilantro leaves, to garnish

PANDI KARI

Mangalorean pork curry SOUTH INDIA

This curry from Coorg also works well with lamb and venison.

Cut the pork into 1-in cubes and place in a shallow dish. Sprinkle with the salt, turmeric, and vinegar and set aside to marinate for 30 minutes.

In the meantime, soak the tamarind in ⅔ cup warm water for 20 minutes, then strain through a fine strainer and set aside.

Transfer the pork and marinade to a heavy-based pan, add 1 cup water, and bring to a simmer. Cook gently for about 20 minutes.

Meanwhile, whiz the cilantro, chili peppers, coconut, ginger, garlic, curry leaves, and mango together in a blender or mini-processor to a fine paste.

Heat the oil in a deep sauté pan and sauté the mustard seeds until they crackle. Add the chopped onions and sauté until softened and light brown.

Add the pork, with its liquid, and cook for 15 minutes. Add the cilantro and coconut paste, and cook on a low heat for a further 5 minutes. Add the tamarind liquid and cook for another 5 minutes or until the pork is done. Adjust the seasoning. Scatter with the fried curry leaves and serve with rice.

1 lb 2 oz lean boneless pork loin or butt
1 tsp salt
1 tsp ground turmeric
2 tbsp vinegar
4 tbsp tamarind pulp*
½ cup cilantro leaves, roughly chopped
2 green chili peppers
5 tbsp grated fresh coconut*
3 tbsp roughly chopped ginger
8 garlic cloves, peeled
20 curry leaves*, plus an extra 10 deep-fried
  leaves to garnish
2 tbsp mango flesh, or 2 tsp mango powder*
4 tbsp vegetable oil
½ tsp black mustard seeds
1 cup chopped onions

VEGETABLES AND LEGUMES

With a population that's over 80% vegetarian, a climate that promotes vegetables and legumes, and strong regional influences, it is not surprising that India's vegetarian cuisine is so rich and varied. Basic vegetables are cooked in hundreds of different ways across India, and in markets you find exotic varieties, such as drumsticks, gourds, and unusual greens that are little known outside India. To me, vegetarian cooking is particularly challenging because the flavors are delicate, so the spicing must be very carefully balanced. Here is a spectrum of vegetable dishes from the different regions.

SING VATANA BATATA

Drumstick, pea, and potato curry KHOJA, WEST INDIA

Drumsticks are a common vegetable in India. They look like long ridged beans (see photograph on page 104), but they are actually the unripe seed pods of a tree native to northwest India. Unfortunately, they may be hard to find in western markets. If you are unfamiliar with drumsticks, the way to savor them is to suck the pulp from the pods, then discard them – rather than eat them whole like beans. If you cannot find drumsticks, use green beans instead – I have found these work well with this recipe.

Cut the drumsticks into 1-in lengths. Blanch the fresh peas in boiling salted water for 3–4 minutes, then drain. Cut the potatoes into wedges.

Put all the ingredients for the spice paste in a blender or mini-processor and whiz to a fine paste.

Heat the 2 tbsp oil in a wok or kadhai. Add the mustard seeds and curry leaves and sauté until they crackle, then add the spice paste and sauté for 3–4 minutes until the oil separates.

Add the drumsticks and potatoes, sauté for a few minutes, then add 7 tbsp water and season with salt. Simmer for 20 minutes or until the drumsticks and potatoes are just cooked. Add the blanched (or frozen) peas and simmer for 2–3 minutes until tender. Serve hot.

7oz drumsticks

²/₃ cup shelled fresh peas, or frozen peas

salt

4 small new potatoes, scrubbed

2 tbsp oil

1 tsp black mustard seeds

10 curry leaves*

SPICE PASTE:

²/₃ cup grated fresh coconut*

2 tbsp chopped cilantro leaves

3 medium tomatoes

2 garlic cloves, peeled

2 tsp chopped ginger

1 tbsp oil

1 tsp Kashmiri red chili powder*

¹/₂ tsp ground coriander

¹/₂ tsp ground cumin

¹/₂ tsp ground turmeric

BEGUN PORA

Roasted eggplant mash BENGAL, EAST INDIA

This flavored eggplant mash makes a great accompaniment to any spicy curry; it can also be served chilled as a salad. At my restaurant, I serve it with my favorite lamb rack roast – it's a perfect match.

Preheat the oven to 400°F (360°F convection oven). Brush the eggplant with a little of the oil and roast in the hot oven for about 15–20 minutes until the skin is charred and peels off easily. Leave until the eggplant is cool enough to handle, then peel away the skin, chop the pulp, and tip into a bowl. Add the remaining oil and mash roughly, using a fork.

Add the onion, ginger, chili pepper, cumin seeds, and salt, and mix well. Finally add the lime juice and chopped cilantro, and toss to mix. Serve warm or chilled.

1 eggplant, about 14oz

3 tbsp vegetable oil or olive oil

¹/₂ medium onion, finely chopped

1 tsp finely chopped ginger

1 green chili pepper, finely chopped

¹/₂ tsp toasted cumin seeds, crushed

¹/₂ tsp salt, or to taste

1 tbsp lime juice

1 tbsp finely chopped cilantro leaves

KALLA VEETU KATHRIKKAI

Chettiar eggplant curry TAMIL NADU, SOUTH INDIA

As a child, I hated eating eggplant in curry form, then I was introduced to this recipe in southern India at my hostel cafeteria – and loved it. The amazing combination of flavors enhances mild eggplant delightfully.

Cut the baby eggplants in half lengthwise. Cut the potatoes into wedges and parboil in salted water for 8–10 minutes, then drain.

Meanwhile, heat the oil in a wok or kadhai and sauté the cassia or cinnamon, fennel seeds, and curry leaves for a minute or two until they crackle. Add the onions and garlic, and sauté until the onions are softened and browned, then add the crushed chili peppers and coriander seeds and sauté for 1–2 minutes.

Add the eggplants and potatoes, and cook for few minutes until the eggplants soften. Add the tomato, coconut milk, 7 tbsp water, and salt to taste. Bring to a simmer and cook gently for about 10 minutes until the vegetables are cooked and the sauce has thickened.

Scatter with chopped cilantro leaves to serve.

8–10 baby eggplants

3 medium potatoes

salt

4 tbsp vegetable oil

2-in piece cassia bark or cinnamon stick

1 tsp fennel seeds

8 curry leaves*

2 large onions, finely chopped

1½ tsp finely chopped garlic

10 small dried red Kashmiri chili peppers*, crushed

3 tbsp toasted coriander seeds, crushed

1 large tomato, cut into wedges

1⅔ cups coconut milk*

2 tbsp chopped cilantro leaves

DAHAIWALE ALOO GOBI

Cauliflower and potato curry BIHAR, EAST INDIA

Cooking with yogurt is an ancient technique in India. I have fond memories of this recipe – the *littee* vendor in my home town sold an exceptionally good version. Indeed *littee* (page 16) are an excellent accompaniment, perfect for mopping up the delicious cooking liquor.

Cut the potatoes into wedges. Cut the cauliflower into small florets. Heat the oil in a sauté pan and lightly fry the potato wedges and cauliflower, turning, for 3–5 minutes. Remove and set aside.

Add the nigella or onion seeds, cloves, cardamom pods, cassia or cinnamon, and bay leaf to the oil remaining in the pan, and sauté for a minute or two until the spices crackle.

Return the potatoes and cauliflower to the pan and add the turmeric, chili powder, salt, and sugar. Mix well and add 1¼ cups water. Bring to a boil, lower the heat, and simmer for about 20 minutes until the potatoes are just cooked.

Add the tomatoes and yogurt, bring to a simmer, and cook for 5 minutes. Add the chopped cilantro and sprinkle with garam masala to serve.

2 medium potatoes, peeled

1 medium cauliflower, trimmed

3 tbsp vegetable oil or mustard oil

1 tsp nigella seeds* or onion seeds

2 cloves

2 cardamom pods*

1-in piece cassia bark or cinnamon stick

1 bay leaf

1 tsp ground turmeric

½ tsp Kashmiri red chili powder*

1 tsp salt

1 tsp sugar

2 medium tomatoes, cut into wedges

¾ cup plain yogurt, lightly whisked

1 tbsp cilantro leaves, finely chopped

½ tsp garam masala

KEERAI PORIYAL

Stir-fried spinach   SOUTH INDIA

In Tamil Nadu, *arrakeerai* and *sirukeerai* are the two greens stir-fried in this way, but the result is equally good with plain spinach. The equivalent dishes in Kerala are called *thoran*. The principle is the same, though the *thoran* seasoning technique is a little different.

Wash the spinach, drain well, and shred the leaves; set aside.

Heat the oil in a wok or kadhai, and sauté the mustard seeds and black gram with the garlic and whole red chili peppers until they crackle. Add the chopped onion and sauté until translucent and softened.

Add the shredded spinach and season with salt. Cook on a low heat for a few minutes until the spinach is just wilted and any liquid has evaporated. Sprinkle with the grated coconut to serve.

1¼ lb spinach leaves

1 tbsp vegetable oil

½ tsp black mustard seeds

½ tsp split black gram*

6 garlic cloves, finely chopped

2 small dried red Kashmiri chili peppers*

1 small onion, finely chopped

½ tsp salt, or to taste

3 tbsp grated fresh coconut*

SAAG PANEER

Spinach with fried paneer   NORTH INDIA

***Saag paneer* is a special winter preparation in north Indian homes, reserved for visiting guests. This recipe is a source of pride, so if you happen to be that lucky guest, don't compare it to other *saag paneers* you have tasted – you would be asking for trouble.**

Wash the spinach, drain well, and roughly chop the leaves; set aside. Cut the paneer into ¾-in cubes. Heat the oil for deep-frying in a large, deep pan to 360°F, and deep-fry the paneer cubes in batches for about 1 minute to seal and lightly color the surface. Drain on paper towel.

Heat the butter and 2 tbsp oil in a sauté pan, add the garlic, and sauté for 1–2 minutes until golden brown. Add the cumin seeds and sauté for a minute until they start crackling. Add the chili powder and coriander and stir for a further 1 minute.

Add the spinach and cook over a low heat for 10 minutes, stirring constantly until the leaves wilt.

Add the paneer cubes, ginger, and salt, and cook slowly for 5–7 minutes. As the oil starts to shine on the surface of the spinach, stir in the cream.

Sprinkle with garam masala and serve garnished with tomato strips.

2¼ lb spinach leaves

10oz paneer cheese (see note on page 31)

2 tbsp vegetable oil, plus oil to deep-fry

2 tbsp butter

2 tsp finely chopped garlic

1 tsp cumin seeds

1 tsp Kashmiri red chili powder*

1 tsp ground coriander

2 tsp finely chopped ginger

1 tsp salt

2 tbsp whipping cream

1 tsp garam masala

1 medium tomato, cut into thin strips, to garnish

SINGHORA DIYE KOLMI SAAG BHAJI

Sautéed watercress with water chestnuts EAST INDIA

Watercress and water chestnuts are both abundant in the markets of Calcutta. Their flavors and textures marry perfectly, giving a natural spicy edge. This recipe is probably the result of neighboring influences on Bengali cuisine from countries like Mynamar, and the Chinese community of Calcutta.

Rinse the watercress, pat dry, and set aside. Heat the oil in a wok or kadhai. Add the nigella and fennel seeds and sauté until they crackle, then add the garlic and sauté briefly until light brown in color.

Add the water chestnuts and sauté for 1 minute, then stir in the turmeric and chili powder. Add the watercress to the pan with the salt. Cook on a low heat for a minute, until the leaves just wilt. Serve immediately.

1lb 2oz watercress, tough stalks removed

1 tbsp mustard oil or vegetable oil

½ tsp nigella seeds*

¼ tsp fennel seeds

2 garlic cloves, crushed

1¾ cups canned water chestnuts, drained and sliced

¼ tsp ground turmeric

¼ tsp Kashmiri red chili powder*

½ tsp salt, or to taste

DHAROSH CHACHHARI

Spicy dry okra EAST INDIA

Cooking with mustard paste and mustard oil is an acquired taste, but one you can easily take on. Either use an authentic Indian mustard paste or buy one of the milder mustard pastes available – for a similar flavor with less pungency. This dish can be garnished with crisp-fried okra if you like.

Slit the okra from tip to tail and set aside. Soak the tamarind pulp in 3 tbsp warm water for 20 minutes, then strain through a fine strainer.

Heat the oil in a wok or kadhai, add the onion seeds, and sauté until they crackle. Add the okra and sauté for a minute.

Add the chili powder, turmeric, salt, and sugar. Cook over a low heat for 12–15 minutes until the okra is tender. Mix the mustard paste with the tamarind liquid, and add to the pan. Cook, stirring gently, for 2–3 minutes, then check the seasoning and serve.

1lb 2oz okra, washed

1 tbsp tamarind pulp*

2 tsp vegetable or mustard oil

¼ tsp onion seeds

1 tsp Kashmiri red chili powder*

1 tsp ground turmeric

½ tsp salt, or to taste

¼ tsp sugar

2 tsp mustard seed paste*, or Dijon mustard

CHINA BODAM DIYE LAL SAAG

Red chard with coriander and peanuts CALCUTTA, EAST INDIA

A variety of red spinach is sold in Calcutta's vegetable markets. Red chard is a good alternative and works very well in this recipe.

Remove the stems from the chard or spinach and wash the leaves; drain well. Lightly toast the coriander seeds and dried red chili pepper together in a small heavy-based frying pan over a medium heat for a minute or two until they begin to crackle, shaking the pan constantly. Crush finely, using a mini-processor or mortar and pestle.

Heat the mustard oil in a wok or deep sauté pan, add the crushed coriander and chili mixture, and sauté for 1 minute. Add the chopped garlic and sauté until golden brown in color.

Add the sliced onion and sauté until softened, then add the tomatoes, stir, and add the turmeric. Cook on a low heat for a couple of minutes.

Add the chard or spinach leaves to the pan with the salt and cook on a low heat for a few minutes until all the moisture has evaporated and the chard leaves start to wilt. Add the crushed peanuts, toss to mix, and remove from the heat. Serve at once.

1¾ lb young red chard or spinach leaves

1½ tsp coriander seeds

1 small dried red Kashmiri chili pepper*

2 tbsp mustard oil or vegetable oil

1 garlic clove, chopped

1 medium onion, finely sliced

3 medium tomatoes, chopped

1 tsp ground turmeric

½ tsp salt, or to taste

2 tbsp unsalted peanuts, toasted and crushed

MUTTAKOS KARAT THOREN

Stir-fried cabbage and carrot with coconut SOUTH INDIA

Thoran, poriyal, kaalan, palya, and foogath are simply different names used to describe this kind of dish in different parts of India. The principles of cooking and spicing are similar. All are vegetable-based and feature coconut, curry leaves, and mustard seeds. Perhaps they are best described as warm salads. Fresh coconut is essential here.

Shred the cabbage and grate the carrots or cut into julienne; set aside.

Heat the oil in a wok or kadhai. Add the mustard seeds and, as they splutter, add the black gram and fry until golden brown in color. Add the sliced onion, green chilies, and curry leaves, and sauté until the onion is softened and translucent.

Add the grated coconut and sauté lightly, without coloring, to extract the flavor. Add the shredded cabbage, carrot, bean sprouts if using, and salt. Cook gently for 10–15 minutes until the vegetables are just cooked. Serve immediately.

14oz white cabbage, cored

1 medium or 2 small carrots

2 tbsp vegetable oil

1 tsp black mustard seeds

2 tsp black gram*

1 medium onion, thinly sliced

2 green chili peppers, slit lengthwise

10 curry leaves*

2 cups grated fresh coconut*

½ cup bean sprouts (optional)

½ tsp salt, or to taste

FULAVER GAJJAR VATANA NU SHAK

Spiced cauliflower, carrots and peas GUJARAT, WEST INDIA

Among Indian regional cuisine, I believe Gujarati food stands out for its ingenious spicing techniques, and the melange of colors and textures. This recipe is a regular feature in Gujarati homes – its simple, bold flavors shine through perfectly.

Cut the cauliflower into small florets. If using fresh peas, blanch in boiling salted water for 3–4 minutes, then drain. Blanch the diced carrots in boiling water for 3 minutes; drain.

Meanwhile, heat the oil in a wok or kadhai. Add the asafoetida and mustard seeds, and sauté for a minute or two until the seeds splutter. Add the green chilies, cauliflower florets, and ½ tsp salt. Cook over a low heat for about 10 minutes until the cauliflower stems soften. Add the blanched (or frozen) peas, carrots, and ground spices. Cook for a few minutes until the vegetables are tender.

Serve in warm bowls, scattered with shredded cilantro leaves, and accompanied by Indian breads.

10oz cauliflower, trimmed
⅔ cup shelled fresh peas, or frozen peas
salt
¾ cup diced carrots
2 tbsp vegetable oil
pinch of asafoetida*
½ tsp black mustard seeds
2 green chili peppers, slit lengthwise
¼ tsp ground cumin
¼ tsp ground coriander
½ tsp Kashmiri red chili powder*
½ tsp ground turmeric
2 tbsp shredded cilantro leaves

PATTAR KOLU ANE GUVAR FALI NU SHAK

Pumpkin and bean curry GUJARAT, WEST INDIA

The sweet flavors of the vegetables are perfectly balanced by the spices in this recipe. If you are not keen on cluster beans, you could use green beans instead.

Cut the pumpkin into 1-in long batons. Cut the cluster or green beans into 1-in lengths.

Bring 1 cup water to a boil in a pan. Add the pumpkin, beans, oil, and salt. Bring to a boil, lower the heat, and simmer for about 3–5 minutes until the beans are just softened.

Add the ground spices and jaggery, and continue to cook on a low heat for 2–3 minutes until the vegetables are tender. Serve sprinkled with chopped cilantro leaves.

7oz yellow pumpkin, skin and seeds removed
3½ oz cluster beans or green beans
2 tbsp vegetable oil
½ tsp salt, or to taste
½ tsp ground turmeric
½ tsp Kashmiri red chili powder*
½ tsp ground cumin
½ tsp ground coriander
1½ tbsp jaggery* (palm sugar)
2 tsp chopped cilantro leaves

ALOO PIAJ KOLI O TOMATOR TORKARI

Green onions with potatoes and tomatoes EAST INDIA

This recipe is a prime example of minimalist Bengali cooking. Small amounts of spices are used, so the fresh flavors of the vegetables and cilantro shine through. No water is added to this dish.

Cut the green onions into 2-in lengths and set aside.

Heat the mustard oil in a wok or deep frying pan to smoking point, then reduce the heat to medium and add the panch phoran. Stir for 1 minute or until the spices change color, then add the potatoes and sliced onions. Cook, stirring, for 2–3 minutes, then add the tomatoes.

Sprinkle in the turmeric, salt, and sugar, stir well, and reduce the heat to low. Cover the pan and cook for 8–10 minutes, until the potatoes are almost cooked.

Add the green onions and cook for a further 3–5 minutes until the green onions and potatoes are tender and the oil starts to separate. Serve garnished with cilantro sprigs.

1 bunch of green onions, trimmed

2 tbsp mustard oil or vegetable oil

1 tsp panch phoran*

20 small new potatoes, quartered

2 medium onions, thinly sliced

2 medium tomatoes, thinly sliced

1 tsp ground turmeric

1 tsp salt, or to taste

$^1/_2$ tsp sugar

cilantro sprigs, to garnish

TETUL DIYE SHEEMER TORKARI

Fava beans with tamarind BENGAL, EAST INDIA

Fava beans are an everyday vegetable in west Bengal. This is a recipe with minimal cooking and spicing, and it's therefore fast to prepare. Indian fava beans have softer pods than those generally available in this country and they can be cooked whole. You may be lucky enough to find tender fava beans in pods early in the season, otherwise substitute green beans for this recipe.

Blanch the fava beans in boiling salted water for about 3–4 minutes until *al dente*. Drain and immerse the beans in a bowl of ice water to refresh. When cold, remove and set aside. Soak the tamarind pulp in 6 tbsp warm water for 20 minutes, then strain through a fine strainer.

Heat the mustard oil in a wok or deep frying pan. Add the nigella and cumin seeds, and sauté until they crackle. Add the sliced green chilies and ginger strips, and sauté until the chilies have softened.

Add the sliced fava or green beans and sauté for 1 minute, then sprinkle in the turmeric, sugar, and salt to taste, and cook for another minute. Add the tamarind liquid and stir well. Serve garnished with ginger julienne.

14oz young fava beans in the pod, or
    green beans, sliced diagonally

salt

2 tbsp tamarind pulp*

2 tbsp mustard oil or vegetable oil

½ tsp nigella seeds*

½ tsp cumin seeds

2 green chili peppers, sliced diagonally

1½-in piece ginger, peeled and cut into thin strips

½ tsp ground turmeric

2 tsp sugar

ginger julienne, to garnish

KANDE KI SUBJI

Spicy onions   RAJASTHAN, NORTH INDIA

In Rajasthan, onion is an essential food and it is cooked in various ways. This simple recipe makes a great accompaniment to almost any meal. Serve an Indian bread alongside.

Cut the red and white onions into thick slices. Cut the white part of the green onions into thick strips. Cut the green part into julienne and set aside for the garnish.

Heat the 3 tbsp oil in a wok or kadhai and sauté the cumin seeds until they splutter. Add the ginger-garlic paste and sauté for 2–3 minutes until well cooked.

Add the chili powder, ground spices, salt, 3 tbsp water, and the yogurt. Cook this mixture well, stirring, for 3–4 minutes, then add the onions, including the white parts of the green onions, and stir-fry for about 5–7 minutes until they are just cooked, but retaining a bite.

In the meantime, heat the oil for deep-frying in a deep-fryer or other suitable pan to 360°F, and deep-fry the julienned green onion tops for about 20–30 seconds until crisp. Drain on paper towel.

Serve the onions in bowls, topped with the fried green onion tops.

5½ oz white onions

5½ oz red onions

3½ oz green onions, trimmed

3 tbsp vegetable oil, plus oil to deep-fry

½ tsp cumin seeds

2 tsp ginger-garlic paste*

1 tsp Kashmiri red chili powder*

1 tsp ground coriander

½ tsp ground turmeric

½ tsp salt, or to taste

2 tbsp plain yogurt

DHANIYAE AUR PYAZ KI KHUMBI

Mushrooms with coriander   NORTH INDIA

I must have inherited my love of mushrooms from my mother; this is her recipe and I have eaten it zillions of times. She makes it with white mushrooms and *dhingri* (Indian shiitake), but I use a mixture of varieties. It is an ideal accompaniment to many chicken dishes.

Slice the mushrooms and cut the green onions into julienne strips.

Heat 2 tbsp oil in a sauté pan, add half of the chopped garlic, and sauté for 2 minutes until light brown in color. Add the coriander seeds and dried red chili, and sauté for a minute, then add the tomatoes and salt. Cook for about 10 minutes until the tomatoes are just softened.

Heat the remaining 1 tbsp oil in a wok and sauté the rest of the garlic for 1–2 minutes. Add the mushrooms and green onions, and sprinkle with the turmeric and black pepper. Sauté for 3–4 minutes, until the mushrooms just soften. Add the tomato mixture and sauté for a further 3–4 minutes. Serve at once, sprinkled with cilantro leaves.

14oz mixed mushrooms (shiitake, oyster, chestnut, white, etc)

4 green onions, white part only

3 tbsp vegetable oil

2 tsp finely chopped garlic

1 tsp coriander seeds, crushed

1 small dried red Kashmiri chili pepper*, crushed

2 medium tomatoes, finely chopped

½ tsp salt, or to taste

½ tsp ground turmeric

¼ tsp black peppercorns, crushed

3 tbsp cilantro leaves

SHALGAM MASALA

Turnips with ginger and nigella seeds — PUNJAB, NORTH INDIA

Baby turnips are used as a salad ingredient in Punjabi villages, along with mooli (daikon) and carrots. These root vegetables are used in various forms in India; they are even sun-dried to ensure a year-round supply. I came across a recipe like this made with large turnips and promptly turned it into a baby turnip recipe; it works well and doesn't require lengthy cooking.

Cut the baby turnips into quarters. Heat the oil in a sauté pan, add the nigella seeds, green chili pepper, and ginger, and sauté for 1–2 minutes until the seeds crackle.

Add the turnips and ground spices, and sauté over a low heat for 3 minutes. Add the chopped tomato and salt. Cover and cook until the turnips are soft.

Sprinkle the garam masala, chopped cilantro, and ginger julienne over the turnips and serve.

10oz baby turnips, cleaned
2 tbsp vegetable oil
1 tsp nigella seeds*
1 green chili pepper, chopped
½ tsp chopped ginger
1 tsp ground turmeric
¼ tsp Kashmiri red chili powder*
1 tsp ground coriander
1 medium tomato, chopped
½ tsp salt, or to taste
¼ tsp garam masala
1 tbsp chopped cilantro leaves
2 tsp ginger julienne

GANTH GOBI

Kashmiri kohlrabi   NORTH INDIA

Kohlrabi is a common vegetable in Kashmir, but not in other parts of India. I have often seen khol-khol, as Kashmiri call it, in New Delhi and Jaipur vegetable markets; I presume locals buy it mainly to prepare salads or pickles.

Peel the kohlrabi and cut into wedges. Heat the oil in a sauté pan. Add the asafoetida and sauté until it sizzles, then add the cumin, fenugreek seeds, and cloves. Sauté for 1–2 minutes until the spices crackle.

Add the kohlrabi and sauté for 2–3 minutes, then lower the heat and add 2–3 tbsp water. Cover and cook for a few minutes.

Add the green chili, ginger, chili powder, ground spices, and salt. Sauté for 30 seconds or so to cook the spices and then add 7 tbsp water. Cook over a low heat for 10–15 minutes until the kohlrabi is soft. Add the sugar and chopped cilantro, and cook until the water evaporates. Serve hot.

1lb 2oz kohlrabi
5 tbsp vegetable oil or ghee*
pinch of asafoetida*
½ tsp cumin seeds
¼ tsp fenugreek seeds
2 cloves
1 green chili pepper, chopped
1 tsp chopped ginger
¼ tsp Kashmiri red chili powder*
1 tsp ground coriander
½ tsp garam masala
¼ tsp ground ginger
1 tsp ground turmeric
½ tsp salt, or to taste
½ tsp sugar
1 tbsp chopped cilantro leaves

ALOO DUM

Potatoes cooked with melon seeds NORTH INDIA

There are numerous different recipes for this dish – this simple north Indian preparation, enriched with yogurt, is from the Mogulai cuisine.

Put the melon seeds or cashew nuts in a bowl, add warm water to cover, and soak for 10 minutes, then drain and grind to a fine paste, using a blender or mini-processor; remove and set aside.

Heat a 3/4-in depth of oil in a pan and fry the onions until softened and light brown in color. Remove with a slotted spoon and drain on paper towel; leave to cool. Add the potatoes to the hot oil and fry for 3–4 minutes until golden brown; remove and drain on paper towel.

Whiz the fried onions in a blender or mini-processor to a paste, add the yogurt, and process until smooth; remove and set aside.

Heat the 3 tbsp oil in a sauté pan and sauté the ginger and garlic until golden brown. Add the ground spices and sauté for a few seconds, then stir in the yogurt and onion paste. Whisk in the seed or nut paste and bring the sauce to a simmer, stirring. Add the potatoes, 2/3 cup water, and salt. Bring to a simmer and cook for 15 minutes or until the potatoes are tender.

In the meantime, toast the ingredients for the spice powder in a heavy-based frying pan over a medium heat for 2–3 minutes until they crackle, shaking the pan constantly. Cool slightly, then grind to a powder, using a spice grinder, mini-processor, or mortar and pestle.

Add the toasted spice blend and chopped cilantro to the potatoes, stir and take off the heat. Serve in bowls, garnished with cilantro sprigs.

2 tbsp melon seeds or cashew nuts

3 tbsp vegetable oil, plus extra to shallow-fry

2 medium onions, thinly sliced

1lb 2oz baby new potatoes, peeled

1 3/4 cups plain yogurt

1 1/2 tsp chopped ginger

1 tsp chopped garlic

1/2 tsp ground coriander

1/2 tsp Kashmiri red chili powder*

1/2 tsp ground cumin

1 tsp salt

1 tbsp chopped cilantro leaves, plus extra sprigs to garnish

TOASTED SPICE POWDER:

3 black cardamom pods*

1/2 tsp fennel seeds

2-in piece cassia bark or cinnamon stick

URULAI SOYIKEERAI VARIYAL

Sautéed potatoes with dill SOUTH INDIA

Dill leaves marry with the spices in this recipe to enhance the flavor of new potatoes. It's a simple, quick dish – perfect instant food.

Parboil the potatoes in salted water for 5 minutes, then drain. When cool enough to handle, peel, and cut into quarters.

Heat the oil in a sauté pan, add the mustard and sesame seeds, and sauté until they splutter. Add the peanuts and sauté until golden brown. Add the onion and sauté until softened and light brown in color. Add the ground spices, salt, and chopped ginger, and cook for a few minutes, stirring and taking care to avoid burning.

Add the chopped tomato and dill, and sauté to allow the dill leaves to blend well with the spices. Add the potatoes and cook for 10 minutes or until they are tender and coated with the spice mixture and dill.

14oz new potatoes, scrubbed

salt

2 tbsp vegetable oil

1/2 tsp black mustard seeds

1/2 tsp sesame seeds

1 tbsp peanuts

1 small onion, chopped

1/2 tsp ground turmeric

1 1/2 tsp ground coriander

1 tsp Kashmiri red chili powder*

1 tsp chopped ginger

1 tomato, chopped

3 tbsp chopped dill leaves

MULANGI KADALAI KOZHAMBU

Radish and chickpea curry — TAMIL NADU, SOUTH INDIA

Mooli or daikon with its fresh peppery taste is a favored vegetable in India. I find it works well with this combination of flavorings.

Drain the chickpeas and cook in fresh water with the bay leaf for 2 hours or until tender, adding salt toward the end; drain. Soak the tamarind pulp in 6 tbsp warm water for 20 minutes, then strain through a fine strainer.

Halve the mooli lengthwise, then cut across into ¼-in thick slices. Heat the oil in a sauté pan and fry the mooli slices until lightly browned at the edges; remove and drain on paper towel.

Add the whole spices to the pan and sauté for 1–2 minutes until they crackle. Add the onion and sauté until softened and golden brown.

Add the ground spices, stir for 30 seconds, then add the ginger-garlic paste and sauté well for 2–3 minutes.

Add the tomato and cook for about 10 minutes. Stir in the tamarind liquid, simmer briefly, then add the coconut milk, chickpeas, and mooli. Bring to a simmer and cook for 3–5 minutes until the mooli is tender. Sprinkle with the chopped cilantro, and serve garnished with extra sprigs.

1 cup chickpeas, soaked in cold water overnight

1 bay leaf

1 tsp salt, or to taste

2 tbsp tamarind pulp*

7oz mooli or daikon (white radish)

2 tbsp oil

2 cloves

1-in piece cassia bark or cinnamon stick

2 green cardamom pods*

1 large onion, chopped

½ tsp ground turmeric

1 tsp Kashmiri red chili powder*

¾ tsp ground coriander

2 tsp ginger-garlic paste*

1 tomato, finely chopped

1¼ cups coconut milk*

1 tbsp chopped cilantro leaves, plus extra sprigs

PAPPU DOSAKAI

Pumpkin with lentils ANDHRA PRADESH, SOUTH INDIA

Cooking lentils with different varieties of squash is common in all four corners of India. Bottle gourd is typically used here, but butternut squash or yellow pumpkin also work equally well. This recipe is from a family in Guntur – home to some of India's finest chilies.

Peel the pumpkin or squash, remove the seeds, and cut into 1-in cubes. Cook the gram (split lentils) in boiling salted water for about 20 minutes, until just turning soft but not completely cooked. Drain off all but a cupful of the water.

Add the green chilies, pumpkin or squash, onions, and tomatoes. Simmer over a low heat for about 10 minutes until the pumpkin turns soft.

Add the chili powder, toasted coriander, turmeric, chopped garlic, and salt, and cook, stirring, for a few minutes. Stir in the coconut and simmer for 5 minutes, adding a little more water if necessary. Add the chopped cilantro and remove from the heat.

Serve in bowls, garnished with fresh coconut slices if you like, and accompanied by Indian breads.

1lb 2oz pumpkin or winter squash
¾ cup Bengal gram*
salt
2 green chili peppers, slit lengthwise
2 onions, finely sliced
2 tomatoes, cut into wedges
1 tsp Kashmiri red chili powder*
½ tsp ground coriander, toasted
¼ tsp ground turmeric
½ tsp finely chopped garlic
4 tbsp grated fresh coconut*
4 tbsp chopped cilantro leaves
thin slices of fresh coconut*, to garnish (optional)

TADKA DAL

Home-style lentils   NORTH INDIA

This lentil preparation is famous for it spicing, but it is the chili and garlic in the seasoning that provide the real kick. An effortless recipe, this requires no planning.

Put the split peas or dal into a saucepan with the salt, turmeric, and 1 quart water. Bring to a boil, lower the heat, and simmer for 15–20 minutes until the lentils are soft.

    For the seasoning, heat the oil in a sauté pan and fry the garlic until light brown in color. Add the chili powder and sauté for a minute. Add the tomatoes and cook for 3–4 minutes, then add the cooked lentils. Simmer for 10–15 minutes.

    Serve the dal hot, sprinkled with shredded cilantro leaves, and crisp deep-fried onions if you like.

1½ cups yellow split peas or channa dal
1 tsp salt
1 tsp ground turmeric

SEASONING:
1 tbsp vegetable oil
1 tsp finely chopped garlic
1 tsp Kashmiri red chili powder*
2 medium tomatoes, chopped

GARNISH:
1 tsp shredded cilantro leaves
deep-fried onions (optional)

CHANNA MASALA

Chickpeas from Punjab PUNJAB, NORTH INDIA

Presoaking dried beans overnight – especially chickpeas, red kidney beans, and lentils – is a common practice in India, to shorten cooking times the following day. This recipe is an all-time favorite in north India. It is usually paired with *bhatura* – a bread similar to naan but deep-fried. I recommend serving sliced red onion, green chili, and mango pickle with this dish, too.

Drain the chickpeas, put into a saucepan, and cover with 1 quart fresh water. Add the tea bag and bring to a boil. Lower the heat and simmer until the chickpeas are cooked, about 2 hours. Season with ½ tsp salt toward the end of cooking. Drain the chickpeas, reserving the liquid.

Heat the oil in a wok or kadhai and sauté the onions until softened and golden brown in color. Add the garlic, ginger, and green chilies, and sauté for a minute or two until the garlic is golden.

Stir in the chopped tomatoes and cook for 10 minutes to soften a little. Stir in the ground coriander, cumin, turmeric, and chili powder, lower the heat, and cook for 2 minutes or until the fat separates out from the mixture.

Add the chickpeas, a little more salt if required, and 1 cup of the reserved liquid. Simmer for about 20 minutes or until the liquid is absorbed. Stir in 1 tbsp of the chopped cilantro leaves.

Add the garam masala, crushed toasted cumin, and coriander seeds. Sprinkle with the lemon juice, ginger julienne, and remaining chopped cilantro leaves to serve. Accompany with bhatura (page 136).

1¼ cups chickpeas, soaked in cold water overnight

1 tea bag

½ tsp salt, or to taste

3 tbsp vegetable oil

4 medium onions, chopped

2 tsp chopped garlic

1 tbsp chopped ginger

3 green chili peppers, sliced

5 tomatoes, chopped

2 tsp ground coriander

1 tsp ground cumin

½ tsp ground turmeric

1 tsp Kashmiri red chili powder*

2 tbsp chopped cilantro leaves

¼ tsp garam masala

1 tsp toasted coriander seeds, crushed

1 tsp toasted cumin seeds, crushed

1 tbsp lemon juice

1 tbsp ginger julienne

AAMER DIYE TAWKER DAL

Spicy lentils with mango BENGAL, EAST INDIA

Lentil preparations are so versatile and so varied within India that there must be millions of recipes based on lentils alone. This recipe is a local favorite in west Bengal's villages. The natural flavor of ingredients is the main play in Bengali cuisine, and that's evident in this simple combination of mango and lentil.

Put the lentils in a saucepan with 3¼ cups water, the turmeric, mango powder or sliced raw mango, and salt. Bring to a boil and simmer for about 15–20 minutes until the lentils, and raw mango if using, are cooked.

Heat the oil in a large sauté pan, add the mustard seeds and, as they begin to crackle, add the green chilies, followed by the lentil and mango mixture. Cook for about 5 minutes until the liquid has reduced slightly.

Serve garnished with chopped cilantro leaves.

1¼ cups split red lentils, rinsed

½ tsp ground turmeric

1 tbsp dried mango powder*, or 2 small green mangoes, peeled and sliced

1 tsp salt

1 tbsp mustard oil or vegetable oil

½ tsp black mustard seeds

3 green chili peppers

1 tbsp chopped cilantro leaves, to garnish

ACCOMPANIMENTS

Bread or rice is always at the heart of an Indian meal. In general, bread is the staple food in the north of India, while rice is more common in coastal India and particularly in the south. India produces various cereals, including corn, millet, and barley, but the most popular north Indian breads – including chapattis and naan – are made from wheat flour. Of course, no Indian meal is complete without a chutney. Indians eat tangy, sweet, or sour relishes with almost every meal and snack. Here you will find a good selection to accompany the appetizers and snacks in the book.

NIRAMISH PULAO

Vegetarian rice — BENARES, NORTH INDIA

I have always liked the food in the city of Benares. It is predominantly a Hindu city steeped in ancient traditions and the food is similarly well established. This interesting rice dish couldn't be easier to make.

Wash the basmati rice in several changes of cold water, then leave to soak in cold water to cover for 15–20 minutes. Drain the rice and set aside.

Whiz together the ingredients for the spice paste in a blender or mini-processor to make a fine paste; set aside.

Heat the butter and oil in a heavy-based pan and add the onions, cassia or cinnamon, cardamom pods, and mace. Fry, stirring, until the onions are softened and golden brown in color.

Add the peas and beans to the pan and sauté for 3–5 minutes, then add the chopped tomatoes. Add the spice paste and cook, stirring, for 2–3 minutes. Add the rice, 1 quart water, and the salt. Bring to a boil, lower the heat, and simmer for about 20 minutes until the rice is cooked and the water is absorbed. Serve hot.

2³/₄ cups basmati rice

1 tbsp butter

2 tsp vegetable oil

1 cup sliced onions

1-in piece cassia bark or cinnamon stick

2 black cardamom pods*

1 mace

1¹/₃ cups shelled peas

7oz green beans, cut into 1¹/₄-in batons

¹/₂ cup fresh chopped tomatoes

1 tsp salt, or to taste

SPICE PASTE:

¹/₂ tsp ground turmeric

1 tbsp roughly chopped ginger

³/₄ cup cilantro leaves

BANGALI PULAO

East Indian pulao — EAST INDIA

This spicy rice preparation is especially popular during the festival of "Durga Puja". It is flavored with an unusual blend of aromatics and spices. I like to serve it with a potato curry flavored with bay leaves.

Wash the basmati rice in several changes of cold water, then leave to soak in cold water to cover for 1 hour. Drain the rice and set aside.

Heat the butter in a heavy-based pan or flameproof casserole and sauté the whole spices, nuts, and raisins for a minute until the spices crackle. Add the rice and sauté for a minute.

Add 3¹/₄ cups water and stir in the garam masala, saffron threads, grated nutmeg, salt, and sugar. Bring to a boil and boil for about 8–10 minutes until the rice on the surface is no longer wet, indicating that most of the water has been absorbed.

Reduce the heat and cover the pan or casserole tightly. Simmer on the stovetop, or place in the oven at 360°F (325°F convection oven) for 10–12 minutes until the rice is cooked.

Uncover, sprinkle with the rose water and kewra, if using, and fork through. Serve, garnished with rose petals and jasmine flowers if you like.

2¹/₄ cups basmati rice

3 tbsp butter

2-in piece cassia bark or cinnamon stick

2 cloves

3 green cardamom pods*

²/₃ cup cashew nuts

3 tbsp raisins

1 tsp Bengali garam masala*

pinch of saffron threads

freshly grated nutmeg, to taste

1 tsp salt, or to taste

1 tsp sugar

1 tsp rose water

1 tsp kewra water or screwpine flower essence*
  (optional)

rose petals and jasmine flowers, to garnish (optional)

ARROZ COM COCO

Coconut rice GOA, WEST INDIA

This is the universal rice for Goans and complements most curries of west Indian origin. In Goa, the local red rice would be used, but I find basmati rice works just as well.

Wash the basmati rice in several changes of cold water, then leave to soak in cold water to cover for 15–20 minutes. Drain and set aside.

Heat the oil in a large heavy-based pan and sauté the whole spices for a minute or two. Stir in the ginger-garlic paste and sauté for 2–3 minutes, then add the onions and cook until softened and golden brown. Add the turmeric and rice, and sauté for 2 minutes.

Stir in the coconut milk, salt, and 6 tbsp water. Bring to a simmer and cook for about 20 minutes until the rice is tender and the liquid is absorbed.

1⅓ cups basmati rice

2 tbsp coconut oil or vegetable oil

1-in piece cassia bark or cinnamon stick

2 cloves

6–8 black peppercorns

3 green cardamom pods*

½ tsp ginger-garlic paste*

¾ cup sliced onions

½ tsp ground turmeric

1¼ cups coconut milk*

1 tsp salt

ELUMICHAMPAZHA SADAM

Lemon rice SOUTH INDIA

Rice is the staple food in the south of India, and there are many interesting rice preparations from the region. With so many tasty ingredients, this recipe is stunning and it goes well with most of the south Indian main dishes in the preceding chapters.

Cook the rice in plenty of boiling salted water for about 20 minutes until just cooked. In the meantime, lightly toast the ingredients for the spice powder in a heavy-based frying pan over a medium heat for 1–2 minutes until they begin to crackle, shaking the pan constantly. Cool slightly, then grind to a powder, using a spice grinder, mini-processor or mortar and pestle; set aside. When the rice is cooked, drain and set aside.

Heat the oil in a heavy-based pan and add the mustard and cumin seeds, black and Bengal gram, dried red chili, asafoetida, and curry leaves. As the mustard seeds pop, add the green chilies, ginger, and peanuts. Sauté for 2–3 minutes.

Add the turmeric, rice, and salt to taste. Stir over a low heat until heated through, then add the toasted spice powder and mix well. Remove from the heat and add the lemon juice. Scatter with chopped cilantro to serve.

1⅔ cups basmati rice

salt

2 tbsp vegetable oil

TOASTED SPICE POWDER:

½ tsp aniseed

2 green cardamom pods*

1 clove

⅜-in piece cassia bark or cinnamon stick

½ tsp poppy seeds

SEASONING (TEMPERING):

1 tsp black mustard seeds

1 tsp cumin seeds

1 tsp each black gram* and Bengal gram*

1 small dried red Kashmiri chili pepper*

½ tsp asafoetida*

10 curry leaves*

2 green chili peppers, chopped

1 tbsp finely chopped ginger

3 tbsp peanuts

¼ tsp ground turmeric

juice of 2 lemons

2 tbsp chopped cilantro leaves

MEETHE CHAWAL

Sweet rice CENTRAL INDIA

Sweet rice is a Muslim tradition in India. Muslim communities in different parts of the subcontinent cook sweet rice for holy festivals, but recipes vary according to local influences. Some are lavish, others – like this recipe – simple, but still delicious. If you cannot find jaggery or palm sugar, substitute raw brown sugar.

Wash the basmati rice in several changes of cold water, then leave to soak in cold water to cover for 15–20 minutes. Dissolve the jaggery or raw sugar in ½ cup water; set aside.

Heat the ghee or butter in a heavy-based pan, add the 4 tsp granulated sugar, and cook to a golden caramel. Carefully add 2¼ cups water, the whole spices, toasted coconut, and fennel seeds, and bring to a boil.

Drain the rice and add to the pan. Cook on a medium heat for 10 minutes or until most of the water is absorbed, then stir in the jaggery water.

Cover the rice with a layer of foil or a damp cheesecloth and seal the pan with a tight-fitting lid. Either cook over a low heat on the stovetop, or in the oven at 360°F (325°F convection oven), for 12–15 minutes. Uncover the rice, fork through, and serve.

1⅔ cups basmati rice

½ cup jaggery* (palm sugar), or raw sugar

3 tbsp ghee* or unsalted butter

4 tsp granulated sugar

2 cloves

4 black peppercorns

2 green cardamom pods*

2-in piece cassia bark or cinnamon stick

¼ cup unsweetened dried coconut*, toasted

1 tsp fennel seeds

CHAPATTI

Basic Indian whole wheat bread NORTH INDIA

Bread is sometimes referred to as the "third hand" in India, especially in the north where it is a staple. Used as a utensil to scoop up sauce or dal, it also contrasts with, and enhances the food. Chapatti is known by various names, including *roti* and *phulka*. It is made with a special whole wheat flour, called *aatta* or chapatti flour – produced from wheat grown in the plains of Punjab, Uttar Pradesh, and Bihar.

Sift the flour and salt together into a mixing bowl. Add 7 tbsp water and mix well until smooth. Slowly knead in an extra 3–4 tbsp water until you have a soft dough. Cover with a damp cloth and rest for 15 minutes.

With floured hands, divide the dough into 10–12 equal pieces and shape into balls. Flatten each ball with the palm of your hand, then using your fingers, press it on a lightly floured surface and roll out to a 5-in disk.

Preheat a flat griddle. Lay a chapatti on the griddle and cook on a low heat for 1–2 minutes until bubbles appear on the surface. Turn and cook the other side for 1–2 minutes, or until both sides are speckled brown. Remove and keep warm, wrapped in a cloth, while you cook the rest.

Serve the hot chapattis smeared with a little ghee or butter if you like.

MAKES 10–12

2 cups chapatti flour* (aatta), plus extra to dust

1 tsp salt

ghee* or butter, to serve (optional)

PARATHA

Flaky whole wheat bread NORTH INDIA

Parathas are made with chapatti dough, which is rolled out in the same way, then layered with ghee or butter, and folded into various shapes. Punjabi parathas are usually round or triangular, whereas those in Uttar Pradesh are often square. In India, parathas are a breakfast item, savored with a vegetable curry, or pickle and yogurt.

MAKES 5–6

2 cups chapatti flour* (aatta)

1 tsp salt

chapatti or all-purpose flour, to dust

3 tbsp ghee* or melted butter

Sift the flour and salt together into a mixing bowl. Add 7 tbsp water and mix well until smooth. Slowly knead in an extra 3–4 tbsp water until you have a soft dough. Cover with a damp cloth and rest for 10 minutes.

Divide the dough into 5 or 6 portions and shape into balls. Flatten each ball with a rolling pin on a lightly floured surface and roll into 5-in disks.

Brush a thin layer of ghee or butter on top of each dough round and dust with a little flour, then fold the dough in half to enclose the butter. Apply another thin layer of ghee or butter and sprinkle lightly with flour, then fold in half once more to form a triangular shape. Press the dough firmly and roll out with a rolling pin, maintaining the triangular shape.

Preheat a flat griddle. Lay a paratha on the griddle and cook on a low heat for 1–2 minutes until bubbles appear on the surface. Turn and cook the other side for 1–2 minutes, or until both sides are speckled brown. Brush with butter and cook on each side for a further 30 seconds or until golden brown. Remove and keep warm while you cook the rest. Serve hot.

POORI

Deep-fried whole wheat bread NORTH INDIA

Pooris are made with the same dough as chapattis, but they are deep-fried into soft, light puffs, which can be eaten plain or stuffed with vegetables. They are typically eaten with a potato curry for breakfast in Indian homes. Pooris are also associated with religious functions and celebrations in India.

MAKES 20

2 cups chapatti flour* (aatta)

1 tsp salt

2 tbsp vegetable oil

vegetable oil, to deep-fry

Sift the flour and salt into a bowl and add the oil. Gradually mix in about 1/2 cup water, to make a smooth, stiff dough. Knead the dough until smooth and pliable, then cover with a damp cloth and leave to rest for 30 minutes.

Knead the dough again and divide into 20 equal pieces. Roll each piece out into a 3-in disk. Heat the oil for deep-frying in a deep-fryer, wok, or deep heavy-based pan to 365°–375°F.

Deep-fry the poori, 2 or 3 at a time, for 1–2 minutes until they puff up. Turn and cook for a further 1 minute. Remove with a slotted spoon and drain on paper towel; keep warm while you cook the rest. Serve hot.

NAAN

Seeded leavened bread

This is the classic teardrop-shaped bread of the north, made from white flour, leavened with yeast, and traditionally cooked in a tandoor.

Sprinkle the dried yeast and sugar into the warm milk in a bowl and set aside for 20 minutes until frothy.

Sift the flour and salt together into a mixing bowl and add the yogurt, yeast mixture, and 2 tbsp of the butter. Knead well to make a smooth dough and put into a lightly oiled bowl. Cover with a damp cloth and leave to rise in a warm place for 3–4 hours until doubled in volume.

Divide the dough into 8 equal pieces, shape into balls, and place on a tray. Leave to rise in a warm place for 10 minutes. Preheat the oven to 425°F (400°F convection oven).

To shape the naan, roll out each ball to a round, and then pull out one side to form a teardrop shape. Brush the surface of each naan with butter and sprinkle with the poppy and sesame seeds. Transfer to baking sheets and bake in the hot oven, in batches, for 4–5 minutes until brown specks appear on the surface.

Variation: Omit the poppy seeds. Brush the naan breads with butter and sprinkle with the sesame seeds and 2–3 tbsp finely shredded blanched almonds before baking.

MAKES 8

1 tbsp active dry yeast

1 tsp sugar

$2/3$ cup tepid milk

$3 2/3$ cups white bread flour

2 tsp salt

2 tbsp plain yogurt

3 tbsp melted butter, cooled

2 tbsp poppy seeds

1 tbsp sesame seeds

BHATURA

Deep-fried bread

This bread is often paired with a chickpea curry – *channa masala* (page 129) – and served as a simple meal. There are several versions of bhatura – this is one of the easiest recipes.

Sift the flour, salt, and baking powder together into a bowl. Add the sugar, egg, yogurt, and 7 tbsp water. Mix together and knead to a soft dough. Knead the butter into the dough. Place in a lightly oiled bowl, cover with a damp cloth, and leave to rest for 2 hours to let the dough rise slightly.

Divide the dough into 12 equal portions and roll out on a lightly floured surface into 4-in disks.

Heat the oil for deep-frying in a deep-fryer, wok, or deep heavy-based pan to 360°–375°F. Deep-fry the bhatura, one or two at a time, for about 1–2 minutes until they puff up. Turn and cook on the other side for about 1 minute. Remove and drain on paper towel; keep warm while you cook the rest. Serve hot.

MAKES 12

$3 1/4$ cups white bread flour, plus extra to dust

1 tsp salt

1 tsp baking powder

1 tsp sugar

1 egg

$1/4$ cup plain yogurt

1 tbsp melted butter

vegetable oil, to deep-fry

GAJJAR KI CHUTNEY

Carrot chutney NORTH INDIA

This chutney has been popular in my restaurant for some time. It goes well with salads and canapés.

Peel and grate the carrots, then spread out on a tray and leave to dry in the sun or in a warm place such as above the stove for 30 minutes to draw out the moisture.

Put the ginger-garlic paste in a square of cheesecloth, draw up the corners, twist together, and squeeze tightly over a bowl to extract as much juice as possible; discard the residue.

Put the sugar and vinegar into a wok, kadhai, or sauté pan over a low heat to dissolve the sugar, then bring to a boil. Add the carrots, ginger-garlic juice, spices, and salt. Bring to a simmer and cook gently for about 1–1½ hours, stirring frequently, until the liquid has almost all evaporated. Add the raisins and simmer, stirring, for a further 5 minutes until the carrots are absolutely dry. Take off the heat and leave to cool.

Transfer the chutney to sterilized jars, cover with lids, and leave to mature for at least 2 days before use. Store in a cool place for up to 4 weeks. Refrigerate after opening and eat within a week.

MAKES 2¼ lb

2¼ lb carrots
1 tbsp ginger-garlic paste*
1½ cups sugar
1 cup white vinegar
1 tsp coriander seeds
2 star anise
1½ tbsp Kashmiri red chili powder*
1 tbsp ground cumin
1 tbsp garam masala
1 tbsp salt
1¼ cups raisins

VENGAYA THUVAIYAL

Onion chutney SOUTH INDIA

This fresh onion chutney makes an excellent accompaniment to appetizers such as *momos* (Indian dim sum, page 16) and *karjikai* (Coorgi vegetable puffs, page 19). In south India it is generally served with rice pancakes and steamed rice cakes, or simply eaten with steamed rice.

Soak the tamarind pulp in 4 tbsp warm water for 20 minutes, then strain through a fine strainer.

Heat 1 tbsp of the oil in a sauté pan, and sauté the dried red chili, green chilies, mustard seeds, black gram, and asafoetida for 1–2 minutes until the mixture crackles. Remove and set aside.

Add the remaining oil to the pan and sauté the red onions until softened and lightly browned. Transfer the onions and spice mixture to a blender or mini-processor, add the cilantro leaves, salt, and tamarind liquid and whiz to a coarse paste. Transfer to a serving dish and eat the same day.

MAKES ½ lb

1 tbsp tamarind pulp*
3 tbsp vegetable oil
1 small dried red Kashmiri chili pepper*
2 green chili peppers, chopped
1½ tsp mustard seeds
3 tsp black gram*
¼ tsp asafoetida*
3 medium red onions, chopped
5 tbsp chopped cilantro leaves
1 tsp salt

DHANIYA AUR MUNGFALI KI CHUTNEY

Cilantro chutney NORTH AND WEST INDIA

This versatile, tangy chutney goes well with most Indian snacks and street foods. It also complements many fish and chicken dishes. For a milder flavor, reduce the number of chilies.

Put all the ingredients into a blender or mini-processor and whiz to a smooth paste. If the chutney is too thick, stir in a little water. Transfer to a serving dish and eat the same day.

MAKES ¼ lb

2 cups cilantro leaves, roughly chopped

4 green chili peppers, stems removed

1 tbsp chopped ginger

2 garlic cloves, crushed

3 tbsp lemon juice

1 tbsp roasted black gram* or toasted peanuts

½ tsp salt

TETULER MISHTI CHOTNI

Sweet tamarind chutney WEST BENGAL, EAST INDIA

The chutneys of east India are amazingly different from those in other parts of the country. Bengalis certainly know how to balance their ingredients to perfection. This is a good accompaniment to fried snacks like samosas, as well as salads and some main dishes. It is prepared for special occasions in east India.

Soak the tamarind pulp in 1 cup hot water for 20 minutes, then strain through a fine strainer into a bowl; discard the residue.

Add the grated jaggery, chili powder, toasted spices, and salt to the tamarind extract. If the chutney is too thick, stir in a little water.

Cool before serving, garnished with chopped cilantro leaves. Eat this chutney on the day it is made.

MAKES ½ lb

5oz tamarind pulp*

⅔ cup grated jaggery* (palm sugar)

1 tsp Kashmiri red chili powder*

1 tsp coriander seeds, toasted

1 tsp aniseed, toasted

1 tsp cumin seeds, toasted

1½ tsp salt

2 tbsp chopped cilantro leaves

DAHI AUR SARSON KI CHUTNEY

Mustard and yogurt chutney SOUTH INDIA

I serve this light, simple chutney with a variety of appetizers. It is always popular.

Whisk the yogurt with the honey, salt, chopped ginger, and mint in a bowl and set aside.

Heat the oil in a pan, add the mustard seeds, and turmeric and sauté until the mustard seeds start to sizzle. Add this spice mixture to the yogurt and mix well. Taste and adjust the sharpness with lime juice if required. Refrigerate and use within a day.

MAKES 1¼ cups

1¼ cups thick yogurt

1 tbsp thin honey

1 tsp salt

1½ tsp finely chopped ginger

1 tbsp finely chopped mint

2 tsp vegetable oil

½ tsp mustard seeds

¼ tsp ground turmeric

1 tsp lime juice, or to taste (optional)

BHUNE TIMATER KI CHUTNEY

Grilled tomato chutney NORTH AND EAST INDIA

This fresh chutney is particularly good with *momos* (Indian dim sum, page 16), but it can be served with many other starters, and as a side dish with chicken, lamb, or fish.

Preheat the broiler to high. Slit the tomato skins to prevent them bursting and place on the broiler rack with the unpeeled garlic cloves. Broil, turning occasionally, until charred all over. Remove and cool slightly.

Coarsely chop the tomatoes and place in a bowl. Peel and chop the charred garlic and add to the bowl with the green chili, ginger, oil, lemon juice, cumin, salt, and sugar. Mix well, then add the chopped cilantro. Refrigerate and use this fresh chutney within a day.

MAKES ½ lb

4 medium tomatoes
4 garlic cloves (unpeeled)
1 green chili pepper, finely chopped
1 tsp finely chopped ginger
1 tbsp vegetable oil
2 tbsp lemon juice
1 tsp cumin seeds, toasted and crushed
1 tsp salt
½ tsp sugar
2 tbsp finely chopped cilantro leaves

TAMOTOR CHOTNI

Tomato chutney EAST INDIA

This tangy chutney complements most Indian snacks and street food.

Heat the oil in a pan, add all the spices with the whole dried chilies, and sauté for 1–2 minutes until they crackle. Add the sugar and vinegar, and slowly bring to a simmer to dissolve the sugar.

Add the tomatoes and salt, and cook on a low heat for about 1 hour, stirring frequently, until the tomatoes break down to a thick chutney consistency. Check the seasoning, then take off the heat.

Spoon into sterilized jars, cool, then seal with lids and store in a cool place for up to 2 months. Once opened, store in the fridge and consume within 2 weeks.

MAKES 1¼ lb

4 tbsp vegetable oil
1 tsp onion seeds
1 tsp fennel seeds
1 tsp cumin seeds
1 tsp mustard seeds
2 small dried red Kashmiri chili peppers*
1⅔ cups jaggery* (palm sugar), or brown sugar
1¼ cups white vinegar
2¼ lb ripe tomatoes
1½ tsp salt, or to taste

LAHSUNI CHUTNEY

Garlic chutney NORTH INDIA

In India, this spicy chutney is traditionally prepared on a grinding stone, but a blender will also do the job.

Put all the ingredients into a blender or mini-processor and whiz to make a smooth paste, adding a little water if required. Store in an airtight container in the fridge and use within 2–3 days.

MAKES ½ lb

7oz (about 1½ cups) peeled garlic cloves
4 tbsp Kashmiri red chili powder*
4 tbsp lemon juice
1 tsp salt

AAM KI CHUTNEY

Mango chutney — NORTH INDIA

An excellent chutney to accompany many of the starters in this book.

Peel the mangoes, cut the flesh from the stone, then grate and set aside.

Heat the oil in a pan and sauté the panch phoran for 1–2 minutes until the spices crackle. Add the sugar and vinegar and slowly bring to a simmer to dissolve the sugar. Add the ginger, salt, and grated mangoes, and cook on a low heat for 30–45 minutes until the mangoes are tender.

Transfer to a sterilized jar, cool, then seal and leave to mature in a cool place for 1 week. Thereafter, keep in the fridge and use within 2 weeks.

MAKES 1¼ lb

2¼ lb large, full-flavored green mangoes

3 tbsp vegetable oil

2 tsp panch phoran*

1 cup raw sugar

⅞ cup white vinegar

⅓ cup chopped ginger

2 tsp salt

AAM AUR KRISHNA KAMAL CHUTNEY

Mango and passion fruit chutney — GOA, WEST INDIA

This is a quick chutney if the ingredients are at hand. My Goan friend, Alphonso Pereira, taught me how to make it. For a thin chutney, add an extra 3–4 tbsp coconut milk.

Scoop the pulp from the passion fruit into a small strainer over a bowl and press with the back of a spoon to extract the juice; discard the residue.

Tip the passion fruit juice into a blender or mini-processor, add all the remaining ingredients, and whiz to a fine paste. Transfer to a bowl, cover, and refrigerate until required. Use within a day.

MAKES 5 oz

2 passion fruit, halved

1 garlic clove, crushed

1 green chili pepper, stem removed

grated zest and juice of 1 lime

3 tbsp coconut milk*

1 tsp jaggery* (palm sugar), or raw sugar

½ tsp salt

⅔ cup raw green mango flesh, roughly chopped

2 tbsp chopped mint leaves

PUDHINAE KI CHUTNEY

Mint chutney — NORTH INDIA

This fresh-tasting chutney complements many Indian snacks and starters. It is very quick and easy to prepare. If you have mango powder in your cupboard, add 1 tsp to the chutney with the chaat masala to enhance the flavor.

Put the mint leaves, cilantro leaves, lemon juice, green chili, red onion, and ginger in a blender or mini-processor and whiz to a smooth paste. Transfer to a bowl.

Stir in the yogurt, chaat masala, chili powder, and salt to taste. Cover and refrigerate until required. Use within a day.

MAKES 10 oz

3⅓ cups mint leaves

1⅔ cups cilantro leaves

3 tbsp lemon juice

1 green chili pepper, stem removed

½ red onion, roughly chopped

1 tbsp roughly chopped ginger

5 tbsp thick yogurt

1 tbsp chaat masala*

½ tsp Kashmiri red chili powder*

½ tsp salt, or to taste

ANARASHER CHOTNI

Pineapple chutney   WEST BENGAL, EAST INDIA

Make this easy chutney to serve with snacks, and as a side dish.

Peel, quarter, and core the pineapple, then finely dice the flesh.

Heat the oil in a pan, and add the bay leaf, cloves, and mustard seeds. Sauté for 1–2 minutes until the spices splutter, then add the pineapple and salt. Cover and cook on a low heat, without adding any liquid, for about 15 minutes until the pineapple turns soft.

Add the jaggery or sugar and 3 tbsp water, stir to dissolve, and cook for about 30 minutes until you have a chutney consistency. Cool, then spoon into a sterilized jar and seal. Keep in the fridge and eat within a week.

MAKES 10 oz

1 medium pineapple

1 tbsp mustard oil or vegetable oil

1 bay leaf

5 cloves

1 tsp mustard seeds

1 tsp salt

1½ cups jaggery* (palm sugar), or raw sugar

CHOTE SANTRAE KI CHUTNEY

Kumquat chutney   NORTH INDIA

I invented this chutney to accompany the crab salad on my menu. It also goes well with many fish dishes.

Put the sliced kumquats in a heavy-based pan with the jaggery, vinegar, cumin and coriander seeds, dried chilies, melon seeds, and salt. Bring to a simmer, stirring, and cook for about 45 minutes – 1 hour until you have a thick chutney consistency.

Allow to cool, then spoon into sterilized jars and seal. Store in the fridge and use within 2 weeks.

MAKES 1 lb 2 oz

1 lb 2 oz kumquats, thinly sliced

¾ cup jaggery* (palm sugar), or raw sugar

⅔ cup white vinegar

2 tsp cumin seeds, toasted and crushed

1 tsp coriander seeds, toasted and crushed

3 small dried red Kashmiri chili peppers*

2 tsp melon seeds, toasted

2 tsp salt

SAEB KI CHUTNEY

Apple chutney   NORTH INDIA

My father taught me how to make this chutney and it has been one of my favorites for a long time. It goes well with chicken and lamb.

Peel, quarter, and core the apples, then whiz to a purée in a blender or food processor. Immediately transfer to a heavy-based pan and add the ginger, spices, salt, sugar, and vinegar. Bring to a simmer and cook gently, stirring frequently, for about 45 minutes until the mixture thickens. Remove from the heat and allow to cool.

Spoon the chutney into a sterilized jar, seal, and store in a cool place for up to 2 weeks. Once opened, refrigerate and use within a week.

MAKES 1½ lb

2¼ lb tart cooking apples

1 tbsp finely chopped ginger

1 tbsp cumin seeds, toasted and crushed

1 tbsp Kashmiri red chili powder*

2 tsp salt

1 cup sugar

⅞ cup white vinegar

DESSERTS

Indian desserts and sweets are more complex and intriguing than most of us imagine, yet sadly this is where many people choose to part with Indian food. I have always featured a varied selection of Indian desserts on my menus, giving them a modern twist to heighten their appeal. From Muslim north to Hindu south, Catholic west to Buddhist east, desserts are influenced by religious festivals, and reflect their extraordinary diversity across the subcontinent. I encourage you to sample the varied recipes in this chapter and explore the intricate array of sweet Indian flavors.

RAVA KESARI

Semolina pudding SOUTH INDIA

This humble pudding is very popular in the south, but you will come across it in different guises all over India.

Heat the oil in a sauté pan, wok, or kadhai and fry the cashew nuts and raisins for 2–3 minutes until the nuts are colored and the raisins plump up. Remove and drain on paper towel; set aside. Drain off the oil.

Heat the butter in the pan and fry the semolina for about 10–15 minutes until golden brown in color, with a nutty aroma. Slowly add 1¼ cups hot water, stirring constantly to avoid lumps forming. Add the sugar, cardamom powder, and infused saffron. Cook gently over a low heat for 5–7 minutes to blend the flavors. Stir in the coconut, cashew nuts, and raisins, then remove from the heat.

Spread the mixture evenly in a greased shallow pan to a 1–1½-in depth and allow to cool, then chill for 1 hour or until set. Cut into triangles or diamond-shaped pieces. Serve cold, topped with a spoonful of shrikhand and plum slices.

2 tbsp vegetable oil

10 cashew nuts

2 tbsp raisins

6 tbsp unsalted butter

1⅓ cups semolina

1 cup sugar

¼ tsp green cardamom powder*

pinch of saffron threads, infused in 2 tbsp milk

2 tbsp grated fresh coconut*, toasted

TO SERVE:

½ cup shrikhand (sweetened thick yogurt, page 148)

1 plum, cut into thin slices

BADAMI PHIRNI

Almond and rice pudding NORTH INDIA

The best *phirni* I have ever tasted was made by Julie Sahni, a friend and celebrated Indian food writer from New York. This recipe is inspired by her.

Put the blanched almonds into a bowl, pour on ⅔ cup boiling water, and leave to soak for 30–40 minutes.

Using a blender or mini-processor, whiz the almonds and water to a fine paste. Strain through a strainer lined with a double layer of cheesecloth into a bowl – squeezing the paste in the cloth to extract as much almond flavor as possible. Mix the rice flour with the almond liquid until smooth; set aside.

Combine the milk, cream, and sugar in a heavy-based pan and slowly bring to a boil. Reduce the heat to a simmer and slowly pour in the almond and rice mixture, whisking constantly to avoid lumps. Cook on a low heat for about 10–15 minutes until the mixture starts to thicken and coat the back of the spoon. Remove from the heat.

Allow to cool completely, then pass through a fine strainer into a clean bowl. Stir in the rose water, cover, and chill for 2–3 hours.

To serve, spoon the mixture into chilled dessert cups. Halve the pomegranates and scoop out the fleshy seeds. Spoon on top of the desserts and sprinkle with chopped almonds and pistachios.

⅓ cup blanched almonds

¼ cup rice flour

1¼ cups whole milk

2 cups light or whipping cream

¾ cup cup sugar

2 tsp rose water

TO SERVE:

2 pomegranates

2 tbsp blanched almonds, chopped

2 tbsp pistachio nuts, chopped

SAEB KI KHEER

Kashmiri apple pudding NORTH INDIA

My trainee chef, Imran Munir, showed me how to prepare this Kashmiri apple pudding. It is wonderfully versatile and complements many other desserts, or it can be served on its own.

Peel, quarter, and core the apples, then cut into wedges. Meanwhile, put 1 cup of the sugar and 2$^1/_3$ cups water in a heavy-based pan and heat gently until the sugar is dissolved. Add the apples, with the cassia or cinnamon, and cook for about 10 minutes until just soft. Allow to cool.

Put the milk in another heavy pan, bring to a boil, and simmer, stirring often, for about 1 hour until reduced to almost a quarter of the original volume. Add the remaining $^1/_2$ cup sugar, infused saffron, cardamom, and apples. Heat, stirring, to dissolve the sugar and mix well.

Take off the heat and stir in the rose water. Allow to cool, then chill. Serve the apple pudding chilled, topped with pistachios and mint sprigs.

2$^1/_4$ lb apples
1$^1/_2$ cups sugar
2-in piece cassia bark or cinnamon stick
6 cups whole milk
pinch of saffron threads, infused in 1 tbsp warm milk
$^1/_4$ tsp green cardamom powder*
1 tsp rose water

TO SERVE:
1 tbsp pistachio nuts, roughly shredded or chopped
mint sprigs, to decorate

KHAJOOR KA KHAJA

Date and orange pastries NORTH INDIA

I have seen these crisp pastries sold in vast quantities during Muslim religious festivals in India. The authentic *khaja* pastry is somewhere between phyllo and puff pastry. Here I have used phyllo and drizzled the date pastries with a citrus cardamom sauce. For a delectable dessert, serve with a spoonful of Kashmiri apple pudding (above).

Mince the dates in a blender or mini-processor, then transfer to a small pan. Add the cumin seeds, orange juice, and 6 tbsp of the melted butter. Cook on a low heat for 15–20 minutes, stirring occasionally. Remove from the heat, stir in the almond paste and orange zest, then set aside to cool.

Brush one sheet of phyllo pastry with melted butter, lay another sheet on top, and brush again with butter. Put two spoonfuls of date filling along one side and roll up the pastry to enclose the filling; twist the ends like a candy wrapper to seal. Place on a greased baking tray and brush with butter. Repeat to make another 3 pastries. Rest in the fridge for 20 minutes.

Preheat oven to 375°F (340°F convection oven). Bake the pastries for 10–12 minutes until crisp and golden brown. Cool on a wire rack.

To make the sauce, put the orange juice, lemon juice, sugar, and cardamom pods in a heavy-based pan. Heat gently to dissolve the sugar, then boil to reduce to a thick syrup. Allow to cool.

To serve, dust each pastry with confectioners' sugar, cut diagonally in two, and arrange on a plate. Drizzle with the citrus cardamom sauce.

10oz pitted dates
1 tsp toasted cumin seeds, crushed
$^1/_2$ cup orange juice
$^2/_3$ cup butter, melted
2$^1/_2$ tbsp almond paste
finely pared zest of 20 kumquats or 1 orange,
    blanched and finely shredded
8 sheets of phyllo pastry, each 8-in square
confectioners' sugar, to dust

SAUCE:
juice of 4 oranges
juice of 2 lemons
1 cup sugar
15 cardamom pods*, bruised

GAJJAR KA HALWA

Carrot halwa   PUNJAB, NORTH INDIA

This irresistible dessert is always in demand in Punjabi homes during the winter months. The authentic version is made with pure ghee, though I prefer to use unsalted butter. It's pure sin food – that's why it is so delicious!

Peel and grate the carrots; set aside. Pour the milk into a large sauté pan or other wide pan, bring to a boil, and simmer, stirring often, until reduced to almost 1 quart; this will take about an hour.

Add the grated carrots to the reduced milk and return to a boil. Reduce the heat and simmer, stirring frequently, for about 1 hour until all the milk has evaporated.

Add the sugar and simmer, stirring, to dissolve. Continue to cook, stirring, until the carrots are quite dry. Add the ghee or butter and sauté well for 20–25 minutes. Stir in the cardamom powder, toasted melon seeds, and raisins, then remove from the heat.

To serve, spoon the halwa into lightly greased 2 1/2-in rings on individual plates. Smooth the surface to shape neatly, then carefully lift off the rings. Top each serving with a spoonful of basundi and a mint sprig. Scatter chopped pistachios around the halwa. Serve warm.

Basundi: Put 2 quarts whole milk in a large sauté pan or other wide pan. Bring to a boil and simmer for about 1 1/2 hours, stirring frequently, until reduced to one third of the original volume. Add 3/4 cup sugar and simmer for 3–5 minutes until the sugar dissolves. Add 1/2 tsp green cardamom powder and 1/4 tsp saffron threads. Serve chilled.

2 1/4 lb carrots

2 quarts whole milk

1 cup granulated sugar

7 tbsp ghee* or unsalted butter

1 tsp green cardamom powder*

1 tbsp melon seeds, toasted

1 tbsp raisins, soaked in warm water for 10 minutes, then drained

TO SERVE:

basundi (see left)

2 tbsp chopped pistachio nuts

mint sprigs, to decorate

SHRIKHAND

Saffron and cardamom yogurt   WEST INDIA

This Indian yogurt can be served as an accompaniment to various other puddings or as a light dessert on its own. In Mumbai, it is relished with poori (deep-fried puffed bread, page 135).

Put the thick yogurt in the middle of a piece of cheesecloth, draw up the corners, and tie together, then suspend over a bowl in a cool place for 2–3 hours to drain off the excess liquid from the yogurt.

Pour the drained yogurt into a clean bowl, add the sugar, saffron, and cardamom, and whisk lightly to combine. Spoon the yogurt into small bowls and refrigerate for 1 hour before serving.

Top with almonds and pistachio slivers to serve.

3 3/4 cups (2 1/4 lb) thick yogurt

3/4 cup sugar

pinch of saffron threads, infused in 1 tbsp warm milk

1 tsp green cardamom powder*

TO DECORATE:

slivered blanched almonds

slivered pistachio nuts

BHAPA DOI E GOOLER MISHTI

Baked yogurt with figs in syrup

This is prepared in a similar way to a *crème caramel*, but without eggs. Indian desserts – including the famous kulfi ice cream – are commonly thickened with *rabari*, or reduced milk, rather than eggs. Here I have cheated slightly and used condensed milk. To balance the sweetness, figs – known as *gooler* or *anjeer* in India – are poached in a spiced lemon syrup to serve alongside. These figs will complement many other desserts, too.

Preheat the oven to 300°F (270°F convection oven). Line four ramekins with paper muffin liners.

Whisk the condensed milk, yogurt, and cardamom powder together in a bowl, then fold in the pistachios and raisins. Pour the mixture into the lined ramekins. Stand them in a roasting pan and pour enough warm water into the pan to come almost halfway up the sides of the molds. Bake in the oven for 40–50 minutes until set.

Meanwhile, prepare the figs. Put the sugar, 1¼ cups water, the lemon zest and juice, and the spices in a small heavy-based pan and place over a low heat until the sugar has dissolved, then bring to a boil. In the meantime, cut each fig vertically into four. Add the figs to the sugar syrup and simmer for 2 minutes, then immediately take the pan off the heat. Leave the figs to cool in the syrup.

On removing the baked puddings from the oven, take the ramekins out of the water, and set aside to cool.

To serve, unmold the puddings onto serving plates, arrange the figs on top, and drizzle a little of the poaching syrup around the plates.

Variation: If figs are out of season, try serving the baked yogurts topped with a scoop of blackberry or raspberry sorbet.

⅔ cup sweetened condensed milk

¾ cup thick yogurt

pinch of green cardamom powder*

1 tbsp pistachio nuts, cut into slivers

1 tbsp raisins, soaked in warm water for 10 minutes, then drained

FIGS IN SYRUP:

4 ripe figs

2 tbsp granulated sugar

finely pared zest of 1 lemon

1 tsp lemon juice

2 cloves

1-in piece cassia bark or cinnamon stick

1 star anise

KAJU KULFI

Rich cashew nut ice cream NORTH AND WEST INDIA

This ice cream originated in north India but it is also very popular in Goa and along the Konkani coast of west India, where kulfi vendors on bicycles are a common sight. Sometimes they sell it with a dipping sauce made with seasonal fruits. Here, I have used raspberries.

Pour the milk into a heavy-based pan, add the cardamom powder, and bring to a boil, then lower the heat. Simmer, stirring frequently, until the milk has reduced to one third of the original volume and has a granular consistency; this will take about 1½ hours.

Take off the heat and stir in the sugar and crushed nuts. Return the pan to a low heat and stir until the sugar has dissolved. Remove from the heat and set aside to cool. Add the kewra water or rose essence, mix well, then cover and chill thoroughly. (If you have an ice-cream maker, churn the mixture for 30–45 minutes at this stage to refine the texture.)

Fill individual conical molds, about ¾-cup capacity, with the kulfi mixture and freeze for 4–5 hours until firm.

To make the sauce, purée the raspberries with the confectioners' sugar in a blender, then strain through a fine sieve into a bowl. Chill until required.

To serve, unmold the kulfi and slice each one into four pieces. Arrange on chilled plates and drizzle the raspberry sauce around. Serve at once.

2 quarts whole milk

½ tsp green cardamom powder*

2 cups granulated sugar

⅓ cup cashew nuts, lightly toasted and crushed

4 drops kewra water (screwpine flower essence)* or rose essence

RASPBERRY SAUCE:

1 cup raspberries

¼ cup confectioners' sugar, or to taste

TANDOORI PHAL

Roasted fruits NORTH INDIA

In India, cooking fruits in a tandoor is a common technique. As a variation on this theme, I marinate the fruits in a spiced honey and yogurt mixture before roasting in the oven or broiling. The result is delicious, and makes an excellent accompaniment to kulfi.

Cut the apples into large wedges, discarding the cores. Cut the pineapple, star fruit, papaya, and mango into slices. Cut the banana into 3 or 4 pieces.

Mix together the ingredients for the marinade in a shallow dish, add the fruits, turn to coat, and leave to marinate for 30 minutes.

Preheat the oven to 400°F (360°F convection oven), or preheat the broiler to high. Put the fruits in a roasting pan, or thread them onto skewers if broiling. Cook in the oven or under the broiler for 7–10 minutes until charred on the surface. Serve warm, with kulfi (above) if you like.

2 apples (1 red, 1 green)

¼ pineapple, peeled and cored

1 star fruit

½ papaya, peeled

½ mango, peeled

1 banana, peeled

MARINADE:

1 tsp toasted sesame seeds

¼ tsp black peppercorns, freshly crushed

¼ tsp green cardamom powder*

1 bay leaf

1 tsp grated lime zest

1 tsp lime juice

2 tbsp thin honey

3 tbsp plain yogurt

MENUS

● **FIRST COURSE** ● **SECOND COURSE** ● **THIRD COURSE**

SIMPLE MENU TO SERVE 3-4

● **ALOO TIKKI** page 23
Pan-fried potato cakes
DAHI AUR SARSON KI CHUTNEY page 138
Mustard and yogurt chutney
● **MEEN MOLEE** page 40
Keralan coconut fish curry
KEERAI PORIYAL page 111
Stir-fried spinach
TADKA DAL page 128
Home-style lentils
ARROZ COM COCO page 133
Coconut rice
● **RAVA KESARI** page 144
Semolina pudding

SIMPLE MENU TO SERVE 3-4

● **FOFOS** page 27
Goan fish croquettes
VELLARIKKAI KOSUMALLI page 32
Cucumber salad
● **CHUTNEY NI MURGI** page 60
Chicken cooked in tangy herb paste
MUTTAKOS KARAT THOREN page 115
Stir-fried cabbage and carrot with coconut
PAPPA DOSAKAI page 127
Pumpkin with lentils
ELUMICHAMPAZHA SADAM page 133
Lemon rice
CHAPATTI page 134
● **BADAMI PHIRNI** page 144
Almond and rice pudding

SIMPLE MENU TO SERVE 4-5

● **PAPARIS RECHEADOS** page 15
Stuffed poppadoms
AAM AUR KRISHNA KAMAL CHUTNEY page 140
Mango and passion fruit chutney
● **ISMAILI MACHCHI CURRY** page 47
Khoja fish curry
MURG HARA MASALA page 72
Herb flavored chicken
BEGUN PORA page 106
Roasted eggplant mash
CHINA BODAM DIYE LAL SAAG page 115
Red chard with coriander and peanuts
BANGALI PULAO page 132
East Indian pulao
PARATHA page 135
● **KHAJOOR KA KHAJA** page 147
Date and orange pastries

MENU TO SERVE 4-5

● **MOMOS** page 16
Indian dim sum
LUQMI page 19
Spicy lamb pastries
TETULER MISHTI CHOTNI page 138
Sweet tamarind chutney
BHUNE TIMATER KI CHUTNEY page 139
Grilled tomato chutney
● **HARI MACHCHI** page 40
Fish fried in green spice paste
CHAAP KARI VARUVAL page 89
Lamb chop curry
DHANIYAE AUR PYAZ KI KHUMBI page 121
Mushrooms with coriander
ALOO DUM page 125
Potatoes cooked with melon seeds
TADKA DAL page 128
Home-style lentils
BANGALI PULAO page 132
East Indian pulao
CHAPATTI page 134
● **SAEB KI KHEER** page 147
Kashmiri apple pudding

MENU TO SERVE 4-6

● **JHINGA TIL TINKA** page 36
Deep-fried shrimp with vermicelli coating
SALADE DE CARANGUEJOS page 36
Crab salad with coconut and curry leaves
● **TENGA** page 44
Sweet and sour fish curry
KOZHI VELLAI KAZHAMBU page 67
White chicken curry
SAAG PANEER page 111
Spinach with fried paneer
ALOO PIAJ KOLI O TOMATOR TORKARI page 118
Green onions with potatoes and tomatoes
TADKA DAL page 128
Home-style lentils
BANGALI PULAO page 132
East Indian pulao
NAAN page 136
● **SHRIKHAND** page 148
Saffron and cardamom yogurt

MENU TO SERVE 4–6

TANDOORI SUBJ CHAAT page 32
Roasted vegetable salad

SHAMMI KEBAB page 24
Pan-fried lamb cakes

PUDHINAE KI CHUTNEY page 140
Mint chutney

NIMBUWALI MACHCHI page 48
Salmon with lime marinade

ACHARI MURG page 71
Rajasthani pickled chicken curry

ALOO GOSHT SALAN page 94
Lamb with potatoes

DHAROSH CHACHHARI page 112
Spicy dry okra

PAPPU DOSAKAI page 127
Pumpkin with lentils

ELUMICHAMPAZHA SADAM page 133
Lemon rice

POORI page 135

BHAPA DOI E GOOLER MISHTI page 151
Baked yogurt with figs in syrup

MENU TO SERVE 4–6

TANDOORI MURG page 71
Tandoori spice roasted chicken

PUDHINAE KI CHUTNEY page 140
Mint chutney

SUNDAL page 35
Chickpea, mango, and coconut salad

CHEMEEN MANGA CHARU page 55
Shrimp and green mango curry

NADIR GADH page 48
Fish curry with lotus stems

KAIRI KA GOSHT DO PIAZA page 90
Lamb in mango and onion sauce

KALLA VEETU KATHRIKKAI page 108
Chettiar eggplant curry

ALOO DUM page 125
Potatoes cooked with melon seeds

BANGALI PULAO page 132
East Indian pulao

PARATHA page 135

KHAJOOR KA KHAJA page 147
Date and orange pastries

ELABORATE MENU TO SERVE 4–6

TANDOORI PANEER AUR HARI GOBI page 31
Roasted paneer and broccoli

PUDHINAE KI CHUTNEY page 140
Mint chutney

CARIL DE CARANGUEJOS page 56
Goan crab curry

HYDERBADI KALI MIRICH KA MURG page 64
Peppery chicken curry

VADAMA KARI KOZHAMBU page 85
Almond lamb curry

KEERAI PORIYAL page 111
Stir-fried spinach

SHALGAM MASALA page 122
Turnips with ginger and nigella seeds

KANDE KI SUBJI page 121
Spicy onions

BANGALI PULAO page 132
East Indian pulao

CHAPATTI page 134

KAJU KULFI page 152
Rich cashew nut ice cream

TANDOORI PHAL page 152
Roasted fruits

ELABORATE MENU TO SERVE 5–7

RAJMA KE GELAWATI page 23
Red kidney bean cakes

FOFOS page 23
Goan fish croquettes

TAMATOR CHOTNI page 139
Tomato chutney

MOCHHA CHINGRI MAACHHER MOLAI CURRY page 55
Lobster curry with coconut

SURTI SANTARA NA CHHAL MA BATHAK page 77
Duck curry with orange

MARATHI NALLI GOSHT page 93
Marathi-style lamb shank

DAHAIWALE ALOO GOBI page 109
Cauliflower and potato curry

GANTH GOBI page 122
Kashmiri kohlrabi

BANGALI PULAO page 132
East Indian pulao

PARATHA page 135

SAEB KI KHEER page 147
Kashmiri apple pudding

KHAJOOR KA KHAJA page 147
Date and orange pastries

GLOSSARY

Aatta or chapatti flour

A type of whole wheat flour used in Indian homes to make unleavened Indian breads. It is made from Indian wheat that is low in gluten and soft-textured. Although aatta is milled to a fine powder, Indians still sieve it, to help aerate and clean the flour.

Ajwain seeds

Greenish-brown seeds with a strong aroma reminiscent of thyme leaves, which may be substituted if necessary.

Asafoetida

A dried gum-like resin, which is also available ground as a powder. It lends an interesting flavor when used in small quantities, but in bulk it releases an overpowering smell. Asafoetida powder contains rice powder to prevent lumping. Use sparingly.

Bengal gram

A type of lentil produced from black gram by removing its dark outer skin and splitting the kernel in two, Bengal gram is widely used all over India and features in a variety of main dishes as well as snack items. It is one of the main ingredients in the popular western snack "Bombay Mix".

Bengali garam masala

The term garam masala generally describes an aromatic blend of several dry-roasted and ground warm spices. Every region in India has a few traditional recipes for garam masala. The composition of this Eastern spice blend varies, but the classic mixture is equal quantities of cloves, cinnamon, and green cardamom with a couple of bay leaves, toasted and ground or blended to a fine powder. You can buy Bengali garam masala from most Indian food stores. Toasted garam masala is always added toward the end of the cooking unless otherwise stated.

Black gram

Confusingly, this is a type of yellow pea, akin to chickpea, with its dark skin removed. It is used in various ways – as a lentil, snack, or flavoring. Black gram can also be sprouted, or soaked then eaten raw in salads.

Cardamom

Available both as pale green and larger, black pods containing seeds, this fragrant spice is often used in Indian dishes. The seeds may be ground to a powder, which is also sold ready-prepared. Green cardamom powder has a particularly fine flavor.

Chaat masala

A beige powdered spice blend with a tangy flavor, which is used as a salad seasoning. It is a mixture of mango powder, black salt, asafoetida, and powdered dried mint. Chaat masala is available from Indian food stores.

Coconut, fresh

Fresh coconut is an important ingredient in coastal India. To extract the flesh from a fresh coconut, push a skewer through the eye of the nut and drain off the liquid, then crack open and remove the brown skin. The white flesh can be grated, shredded, or finely sliced. Fresh coconut can also be deep-fried. You can also whiz roughly chopped coconut in a blender or mini-processor to finely grate it. In this form, coconut freezes well.

Unsweetened dried coconut can be used as a substitute for fresh, but as it has a drier texture, I only use it in toasted form, as an alternative to freshly toasted coconut.

Coconut milk

This is prepared from fresh coconut flesh and shouldn't be confused with the liquid in the shell. To make coconut milk, soak 6 1/4 cups freshly grated coconut in 1 1/4 cups tepid water for 30 minutes, then whiz in a blender on high speed for 3–4 minutes. Strain though a fine sieve or cheesecloth-lined strainer. You should have about 1 cup. This first extract is called thick coconut milk, simply referred to as coconut milk in my recipes.

To make thin coconut milk, soak the residue (from the first extract) in another 1 1/4 cups tepid water and repeat the process.

If you buy cans or cartons of coconut milk, dilute by 5–7% to obtain the right result.

Curry leaves

Used either whole or chopped as a herb in cooking, curry leaves have a fresh taste and aroma, which is rather like curry powder. Sold in bunches, curry leaves freeze well.

Dried red Kashmiri chili pepper

Dried red chili peppers from Kashmir are big and broad. They are used either whole or crushed to a powder. These mild chilies are the best choice for making chili paste to flavor marinades and enrich sauces.

Fenugreek leaf powder

Fenugreek seeds and leaves are two very different ingredients and not interchangeable. Dried fenugreek leaf powder is available from Indian food stores. Alternatively, you can dry fenugreek leaves on a tray in a cool warming oven, or other dry, warm place. Once dry, grind to a powder in a spice grinder, then pass through a sieve. Store in an airtight container to preserve the fragrance and flavor.

Fried onion paste

Made by puréeing deep-fried onions with yogurt, this paste is used as a base for sauces. To prepare, very finely slice 1lb 2oz peeled onions, then deep-fry in hot oil until crisp and brown. Drain thoroughly on paper towel to remove excess oil, then blend with 3 1/2 tbsp yogurt to a fine paste. Store the paste in a jar in the fridge, for up to 2 weeks.

Ghee

This clarified butter has long been the main cooking medium in north India, but with a growing awareness of healthy eating, oil is taking its place. I prefer to cook with vegetable oil and, if necessary, enrich the dish at the end with butter or perhaps ghee. If you want to use ghee, it is available in cans from specialist suppliers.

Ginger paste

To prepare, peel and chop 10oz fresh root ginger and blend with 2 tbsp cold water to make a fine paste, using a blender or mini-processor. Or grate the ginger using a fine grater, then mix with the water. Ginger paste can be frozen in an ice-cube tray.

Ginger-garlic paste

This is widely used. To prepare, blend 1/2 cup each of peeled garlic and peeled, chopped ginger with 1 tbsp water, using a blender or mini-processor. The paste should be smooth and very fine. Store in a sealed jar in the fridge. To keep ginger-garlic paste for longer, add 1½ tsp vegetable oil and 1 tsp lemon juice as you blend the paste. You can also freeze ginger-garlic paste in an ice-cube tray.

Gram flour
Also called besan, this is a fine flour made from ground chickpeas. It is pale yellow in color and has an excellent nutty flavor. Gram flour is used for breads, pancakes, and coating batters for fritters, notably bhajis.

Green chili paste
Green chili peppers range in heat from mild to devilishly hot. Most of their heat is stored within the seeds and white pith or *capillae* holding them in the pod. Removing these seeds and white membrane takes away most of the heat. Green chili paste is used where flavor is required rather than heat. To prepare, seed green chilies and remove all white pith, then whiz to a paste in a blender or mini-processor with a little water and vegetable oil. Refrigerate and use within 3–5 days.

Jaggery and palm sugar
Jaggery is dark, raw sugar from the sugar cane plant. It has a distinctive taste and is less sweet than refined sugar. Palm sugar is made from the sap of various palm trees, such as date, coconut, etc. Both sugars are loosely called *gur* in India. Used to enrich sauces and desserts, they are largely interchangeable in Indian cooking.

Kashmiri red chili powder
Kashmiri chili powder is used in Indian dishes more for its distinctive color and flavor than for its heat. It has a strong flavoring impact on the food it is cooked with, especially when it is sautéed in oil, usually with other flavorings.

Kewra water (screwpine flower essence)
This is a scented flavoring obtained from the flower of the screwpine tree that grows mainly in southern India. Kewra is used in rice dishes, sweets, and drinks.

Mango powder and dried slices
Dried slices of unripe pale mango are used to lend a sour flavor and character to curries, chutneys, and lentil dishes. Dried unripe mango is also available as a powder, known as *amchoor*. It is tangy and sour and used as a flavoring and souring agent in sauces and salad dressings. Both dried mango slices and mango powder are available from Indian food stores.

Mustard seed paste
Mustard paste is an unusual flavoring in Indian cooking and it is generally only used in the east. To prepare an authentic Indian mustard paste, whiz 1 cup black or brown mustard seeds with 2 tbsp water to a fine paste. Store in the fridge for up to a week or, to keep longer, mix with a little vegetable oil.

Nigella seeds
Mild, slightly peppery, black seeds, used as a spice in Indian cooking. Nigella seeds look like onion seeds, but have a different flavor.

Panch phoran
This unique spice mix is particular to Bengal in the north east. It comprises equal quantities of five strongly flavored spices: onion seeds, fennel seeds, fenugreek seeds, cumin seeds, and *radhuni* – a typical Bengali spice. If you can't get hold of *radhuni*, substitute mustard seeds.

Pomegranate seed powder
Sun-dried pomegranate seeds are used to impart a sour flavor to north Indian dishes. They are also available in powdered form from Indian food stores.

Saffron
This is the dried stigmas of the saffron crocus flower. As it takes many of these stigmas to produce a relatively small quantity of saffron, it is an expensive spice, but only a little is required to impart a distinctive flavor and golden hue. I prefer to use saffron threads (also called strands) rather than powdered saffron, which is easily adulterated. To release the flavor, saffron threads need to be infused in warm water or other warm liquid. Lightly toasting saffron threads in a dry pan prior to infusing heightens the flavor. Infuse a pinch of saffron threads (or strands) in 2 tbsp tepid warm milk or water for about 30 minutes, then use as the recipe directs.

Sattu (roasted black gram flour)
This flour is used as nutritious snack. The roasted black gram is ground to a fine flour, then sieved and kept in airtight containers. Mixed with chilled water, it is consumed to cool the body. Mixed with spices it is used as a filling for breads and snacks.

Spices, grinding
This is an essential technique. Depending on the recipe, it may be dry grinding or wet grinding. In India, traditional stone grinders are giving way to mechanical blenders, though these don't develop the same depth of flavor. For dry grinding, use a spice grinder, mini-processor or mortar and pestle. For wet grinding, use a blender or mini-processor. Spices should be ground as specified in the recipe – to a coarse, fine or very fine paste or powder.

Spices, toasting
Toasting spices heightens their flavors. Use a heavy-based frying pan or flat griddle and toast the spices over a medium-high heat, shaking the pan or stirring gently to avoid burning, until the spices pop and develop aroma. Once toasted, spices lose flavor quickly, so toast and use immediately. Sometimes, they are ground before being added to a dish, to bring out their flavor to the full. If possible, pound toasted spices using a mortar and pestle, rather than an electric grinder to retain maximum flavor.

Tamarind pulp
Tamarind is used as a tangy souring agent in Indian cooking. The flavor is derived from the pods of the tamarind tree. These are sold as seedless, dried compressed blocks, each 7oz. This tamarind pulp needs to be macerated in hot water before use. Break up the pulp and soak in hot water for about 20 minutes to soften. Using your fingers, mix the pods with the water – the tamarind paste will become thicker. Strain through a sieve into a bowl, pressing to extract as much flavor as possible. The proportion of liquid to tamarind pulp varies according to the intensity of flavor required. For a thick paste, allow 1¾ cups per 7oz block. This can be stored in the fridge for 2–3 weeks, or frozen, then diluted before use.

INDEX